# FISHING WITH ARTIFICIAL LURES

THE HUNTING & FISHING LIBRARY

By Dick Sternberg

**DICK STERNBERG**, one of the nation's foremost angling authorities, specializes in jig fishing. He has used artificial lures to catch every major type of freshwater gamefish in North America.

**PARKER BAUER**, a freelance outdoor magazine and film writer, is an accomplished multi-species fisherman. An expert in the finer points of artificial lure presentation, he offers many helpful tips to make lures more effective.

**LARRY DAHLBERG** uses flies to catch everything from northern pike and muskies to trout and salmon to bluegills and crappies. A fishing tackle consultant and lure designer, he invented the Dahlberg Diver.

CY DE COSSE INCORPORATED
*Chairman:* Cy DeCosse
*President:* James B. Maus
*Executive Vice President:* William B. Jones

FISHING WITH ARTIFICIAL LURES
*Author:* Dick Sternberg
*Technical Advisors:* Parker Bauer, Larry Dahlberg
*Project Director:* Dick Sternberg
*Production Director:* Christine Watkins
*Art Directors:* Cy DeCosse, Delores Swanson, William Nelson
*Project Manager:* Teresa Marrone
*Researcher:* Joseph Cella
*Director of Photography:* Buck Holzemer
*Staff Photographers:* Kris Boom, Bill Lindner, Jerry Robb
*Studio Manager:* Elizabeth Woods
*Production Staff:* Michelle Alexander, Brian Berkey, Jim Bindas, Julie Churchill, Gerald Krause, Christopher Lentz, Nancy Nardone, Jennie Smith, Bryan Trandem, Nik Wogstad
*Contributing Photographers:* James C. Hodges Jr., Mitch Kezar, John Schneider, Doug Stamm, Dick Sternberg
*Illustrator:* Jon Q. Wright
*Consultants:* Wade Bourne, Mark Hicks, Dick Kotis, Glenn Lau, Ken Menard, Tom Neustrom, Don Oster, C. Boyd Pfeiffer, Don Pursch, Buzz Ramsey, Frank Sargeant, Craig Woods
*Cooperating Agencies and Individuals:* A.C. Shiners, Inc.; Accardo Tackle Co.; Tony Accetta & Son, Inc.; Acme Tackle Company; Nick Adams, Ron Kobes, Lindy-Little Joe, Inc.; Alamance Plastics, Inc.; Fred Arbogast Company, Inc.; Arkie Lures, Inc.; Jim Bagley Bait Co., Inc.; Dan Bailey Flies & Tackle; Bay De Noc Lure Co.; Beaverkill Angler; Jerry Benson; Berkley & Company, Inc.; Big Jon, Inc.; Bill Binkelman Enterprises Inc.; Blakemore Sales Corporation; Blue Fox Tackle Co.; Bobbie Bait Company; Bomber Bait Company; E.F. Brewer Company; Charlie Brewer's Slider Company; Burke Fishing Lures; Cabela's Inc.; Calhoun Beach Club; Ted A. Calvert; Camp Fish; Cannon/S&K Products, Inc.; Ted Capra & Associates, Inc.; Homer Circle; Cisco Kid Tackle, Inc.; Classic Manufacturing Co., Inc.; Robin Coleman, Mepps/Sheldons' Inc.; Cordell Tackle; Creme Lure Company; Dave Csanda, Al Lindner, Jim Lindner, The In-Fisherman; Les Davis, Inc.; Larry Deal; Bill Diedrich; Die Werke International; Do-It Corporation; Dunham's Sporting Goods; Dura-Pak Corporation; Frankie Dusenka, Frankie's Live Bait; Mark Emery; Edward Eppinger; Erie Dearie Lure Co.; Fenwick-Woodstream Corp.; Flagg's Flies; Fleck, Inc.; Fle-Fly Mfg., Inc.; Bob Folder Lures; Bud Glover; Gopher Tackle Mfg. Co.; Paul Grahl, HT Enterprises; Grassl's Double 00, Inc.; Griffin Lures; Gudebrod, Inc.; H&H Lure Co.; Jack Haines; Hal-Fly Tackle Co., Inc.; Bill Hammer, Bill's Jigs; Hanna Lures, LTD.; Harrison-Hoge Industries, Inc.; James Heddon's Sons, Inc.; Tom Helgeson, Bright Waters, Inc.; Helin Tackle Co.; Heluva Lure Corporation; Hi-Fin Tackle Company; The Highland Group; John J. Hildebrandt Corporation; Bob Hobson, Roger McGregor, Alumacraft Boat Co.; Hopkins Fishing Lures Co., Inc.; Odell Johnson; Johnson Fishing, Inc.; K&E Tackle; Clem Koehler, Mercury Marine/Mariner Outboards; Marv Koep's Fishing Pro Shop; Kwikfish Lures, Inc.; Bill Lewis Lures; Lindquist Bros. Bait Co., Ltd.; Lowrance Electronics, Inc.; Luhr Jensen & Sons, Inc.; Lund Lures, Inc.; Lundahl Lures; Mack's Lure Manufacturing; Maxwell MacPherson, Jr.; Mann's Bait Company; Marine Metal Products Co., Inc.; Mar Lynn Lure Company; Martin Tackle & Mfg. Co.; Karl H. Maslowski; Mister Twister, Inc.; Jim Moore, Lund American, Inc.; Motor-Guide; F.J. Neil Co., Inc.; Nelson Marine; Norman Manufacturing Co., Inc.; Normark Corporation; Northland Tackle Co.; O.T. Custom Rodworks; Padre Island Company; Bob Parker; Pelican; Penn Fishing Tackle Mfg. Co.; Steve Price; Prince Mastercraft, Inc.; The Producers/PTC, Inc.; Producto Lure Co., Inc.; Leroy Ras; Rebel; Red Eye Tackle Company; Ric-Jig Tackle, Inc.; C.C. Roberts Company; Bill Rosenbury; Roy's Live Bait; Shamrock Lures, Inc.; Shannon Lure Co.; Jerry Sims; Sims Bait Manufacturing Co., Inc.; Si-Tex Marine Electronics Inc.; Smith Bait Mfg. Co.; Smithwick Lures, Inc.; Snag Proof; Sorel Boots-Sports Sales Inc.; Stanley Jigs, Inc.; Stearns Manufacturing Company; Storm Manufacturing Co.; Strike King Lure Company, Inc.; Super Spawn; The Sutton Company; T's Bass Lures, Inc.; Twist Out, Inc.; Umpqua Feather Merchants; Uncle Josh Bait Company; VMC, Inc.; Vexilar, Inc.; Wade's Custom Tackle; Waldoch Cycle & Sports; Weber Tackle; The Weller Company; Whopper Stopper/Fliptail; Wilderness Enterprises Inc.; Williams Sporting Goods International; Windels Tackle Company; Jack Wingate's Lunker Lodge; Worth Manufacturing Company; Wright & McGill Company; Yakima Bait Co.; Yamaha Motor Corp.

*Color Separations:* La Cromolito
*Printing:* R.R. Donnelley & Sons Company

Also available from the publisher: *The Art of Freshwater Fishing, Cleaning & Cooking Fish, Fishing with Live Bait, Largemouth Bass, Panfish, The Art of Hunting.*

Library of Congress Catalog Card No. 85-70453
ISBN 0-86573-009-1

# Contents

# Introduction

Generations of fishermen have been intrigued with the idea of outsmarting fish with an artificial lure. And nearly everyone who has tossed a lure into the water has fashioned, at least mentally, an improved artificial lure that no fish could resist.

The result of this combined brainpower has been a staggering proliferation of lures in every imaginable shape, size, color and texture. But just when we conclude that it would be impossible to invent anything new, someone designs a lure that outperforms anything currently on the market.

Today's fishermen can choose from a wider selection of lures than ever before. But many anglers fail to take advantage of modern lure technology. Instead, they fish with live bait or use only a few lures that have produced for them in the past.

Even the most accomplished artificial lure fisherman would agree that there are times when live bait is more effective. But artificial lures offer several major advantages over live bait:

- They enable you to cover more water. In most instances, live bait must be retrieved slowly, limiting the area you can cover effectively.

- When the fish are biting, you can catch them more quickly. With live bait, a great deal of time is lost in rigging.

- You can go fishing without first stopping at the bait shop, and you do not face the problem of keeping bait alive.

- Live bait is illegal in some areas, so artificial lures are the only choice.

The purpose of this book is to acquaint you with each major class of lures, show you which lures work best in which situations, and demonstrate the best techniques for using these lures. And, we will show you dozens of little-known tricks that will make your lures more effective.

One chapter is devoted to each of the following lure classes: spinner-type lures, plugs, soft plastics, jigs and jigging lures, spoons and flies. Each chapter contains detailed information on every category of lures in that class. The plug chapter, for example, has sections on nine different categories of plugs including four types of surface plugs and five types of sub-surface plugs.

The book will also help you select the proper equipment for use with each type of lure. Without the right equipment, it would be impossible to present your lures effectively. With the wrong rod and reel, for example, you could not cast far enough or feel the lure working. Line that is too heavy will reduce casting distance, dampen the action of your lure, and possibly spook the fish. Even minor items like snaps or swivels affect your lure's action, so it is important to use the right ones. You will also learn the best knots for use with artificial lures, how to use deep-trolling devices and side planers, and how to enhance your lures with scents.

Whether you're a novice or an expert, this book is sure to expand your knowledge of artificial lures and generate some fresh ideas that will help you catch more fish.

Equipment

# Rods & Reels

Whether or not you catch fish on an artificial lure often depends as much on the equipment used to present it as on the lure itself. And none of your equipment is more important than your rod and reel.

Without the right rod, you could not cast far enough or accurately enough, and you would have difficulty feeling the lure's action and detecting strikes.

Manufacturers generally rate their rods according to the weight of the lures they are capable of casting. Always check the specifications to make sure the rod suits the lure you will be using. Many fishermen carry several rods, each intended for lures of different weights.

Even with lures of the same weight, you may need more than one rod for different methods of fishing and kinds of fish. For example, you could use a one-ounce lure when trolling for salmon with downriggers and when casting for muskies. But downrigger trolling requires a long, limber rod while muskie casting demands a much shorter, stiffer rod. The long, limber rod is necessary for bending into the set position (page 19) and for fighting large, powerful fish on relatively light line. The shorter, stiffer rod is needed to cast the heavy lures and to set the hooks in a muskie's bony mouth.

Another consideration in choosing a rod is its length. A long rod generates more tip speed than a short one, so it can cast the same lure a greater distance. A short rod casts with a flatter trajectory, so it works better for placing your lure under a dock or overhanging tree limb.

Action is also important. A fast-action rod has a stiff butt and midsection, bending most near the tip. This type of rod is best-suited for distance casting because it propels the lure rapidly. A fast-action rod is also best for a solid hook-set.

A slow-action rod bends over its entire length. It is the best choice for accurate casting because it bends

more slowly, giving you more time to aim. And because the lure travels through the air more slowly, you can easily stop it on a precise target. A slow rod is also a better shock absorber, so a strong fish would have more difficulty breaking the line.

Space-age materials and improved rod building technology have resulted in fishing rods that are lighter, stiffer and thus more sensitive than the rods of years past. Graphite and boron rods excel for detecting subtle strikes. They telegraph a lure's wiggle or the beat of a spinner blade better than fiberglass rods. They also help you feel the lure ticking bottom or brushing the weedtops.

The reel you select, whether spinning, bait-casting or fly, must balance with your rod. The sure way to test your outfit's balance is to try casting with it. If the rod feels tip-heavy, the reel is too light. If it feels butt-heavy, the reel weighs too much.

When selecting a spinning reel, make sure that the diameter of the spool suits the line you will be using. The heavier the line, the larger the spool diameter you will need. If you attempt to wind heavy mono on a small-diameter spool, the line will come off in tight, springy coils. As a general rule, use a spool with a front flange at least 1½ inches in diameter for 6-pound mono; 1⅞ inches for 10-pound mono; and 2¼ inches for 14-pound mono.

Spinning and bait-casting reels come with a variety of gear ratios. The gear ratio is the number of times the spool revolves with each turn of the reel handle. On a reel with a gear ratio of 4:1, the spool turns four times while the reel handle turns once.

Reels with large-diameter spools and high gear ratios are needed for retrieving fast-moving lures or large quantities of line. A small-diameter spool and low gear ratio give you more power for reeling in strong fish.

Bait-casting reels should be resistant to backlashing. Backlash-prevention devices like centrifugal or magnetic brakes and *V*-shaped spools will hold the problem to a minimum. Reels with narrow spools work best for casting light lures, but few bait-casting reels can cast lures weighing under ³⁄₁₆ ounce.

Most fly fishermen prefer *single-action* fly reels because they are light, simple and trouble-free. The term single-action means that the spool revolves once with each turn of the reel handle. Multiplying reels have a gear mechanism that boosts the retrieve ratio, an advantage when handling a lot of line or trying to catch up with a fish running toward you. Automatic reels have a spring mechanism for taking up line, but they are heavier, less dependable and have less capacity for line and backing than other types of fly reels.

# Lines

WORLD-RECORD CLASS monofilament is precisely monitored to insure that its breaking strength does not exceed its rating. If the line exceeds its rated strength, a potential line-class record could be disallowed.

One of the most common mistakes in fishing with artificial lures is using line that is too heavy. Always select the lightest line suitable to the conditions. In spinning and bait-casting, heavy line reduces casting distance, is more visible to fish and may restrict the action of your lure. In fly fishing, heavy line makes more splash and may spook fish.

Fishermen who use spinning or bait-casting tackle rely almost exclusively on nylon monofilament line. Mono casts farther than any other line and is less visible in water.

In most fishing situations, use the monofilament that has the lowest diameter for its strength. Most manufacturers list the diameter on the package. Small-diameter line casts better and is less visible than larger-diameter line of the same strength.

## How to Spool on Line

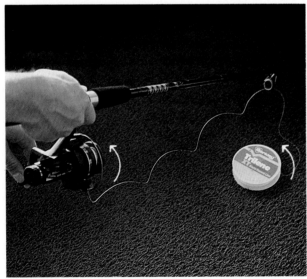

LOAD monofilament onto a spinning reel by taking it off the side of the spool. If the reel turns in a counterclockwise direction, the line must come off the spool in a counterclockwise direction. This method of loading minimizes the twist in your line.

FILL a bait-casting reel with braided or monofilament line by threading your line through the guides, then letting the spool turn on carpet while reeling. Or, simply reel while the spool turns on a pencil. A bait-casting reel will not twist your line in the loading process.

When fishing around weeds or obstructions that could cause fraying, use an abrasion-resistant line. However, these lines usually have a relatively high diameter for their strength. And because of their stiffness, they tend to spring off the spool.

Monofilament is not the best choice for setting the hook in large, hard-mouthed fish like muskies and northern pike. A low-stretch line such as braided dacron works better because line stretch does not dampen your pulling power.

Trollers often use special-purpose lines to reach greater depths or to indicate the depth at which their lure is running. Wire line, either single- or multi-strand, is popular for deep trolling, but it can develop kinks which greatly reduce its strength. Lead-core line will not run quite as deep, but is less prone to kinking. Metered line is color-coded, usually with a different color every 10 yards. When you hook a fish, observe the color on your spool, then let your line back out to that color when you resume fishing.

When choosing a fly line, you must match the line to your rod and to your fly. Although level (L) lines are most economical, double-taper (DT) lines can be cast more delicately, and weight-forward (WF) lines can be cast farther.

Double-taper lines have a long, level section in the middle and an identical taper at each end. They roll over smoothly on the cast and alight gently on the water. When one end wears out, you can reverse the line and use the other end. Double-taper lines are popular for dry-fly fishing, where long casts are seldom desirable.

Weight-forward lines have a short front taper, a thick level section, or *belly,* and a long, thin *running line* at the rear. Weight-forward lines are designed for distance casting but also work well at short range. A special kind of weight-forward line, called a *bug taper,* has a shorter, thicker belly and shorter front taper. Because a bug taper turns over with more power, it works well for casting bugs and other wind-resistant flies.

For even more distance, use a shooting taper (ST) line. The fly line is spliced to a rear section, usually monofilament, called the *shooting line.* An experienced fly fisherman can easily cast a shooting taper over 100 feet.

When fishing on or near the surface, use a floating (F) line. For deeper water, you will need a sink-tip (F/S) or sinking (S) line. Most sink-tip lines have a 10-foot sinking section at the front. The rest of the line floats. Sinking lines enable you to fish deepest because the entire line sinks. But they are difficult to control in current and to lift from the water when you wish to cast.

Always wind on backing before spooling on your fly line. Most fishermen use 50 to 100 yards of 20- to 30-pound braided dacron. Backing insures that a big fish will not run out all of your line. It also prevents your fly line from forming tight coils, as it would if wound directly on the arbor.

*Tips on Caring for Your Line*

RUB silicone fly-line dressing on the front few feet of a braided dacron line. The fraying from constant casting is reduced, so you do not have to trim back line as often.

STRETCH your fly line to remove coils. Tie the leader to a tree, then stretch the entire line. Rub silicone dressing on the floating portion so it shoots through the guides easier.

AVOID leaving monofilament or fly lines in direct sunlight. Prolonged exposure to heat and ultraviolet rays weakens monofilament and cracks the finish on fly lines.

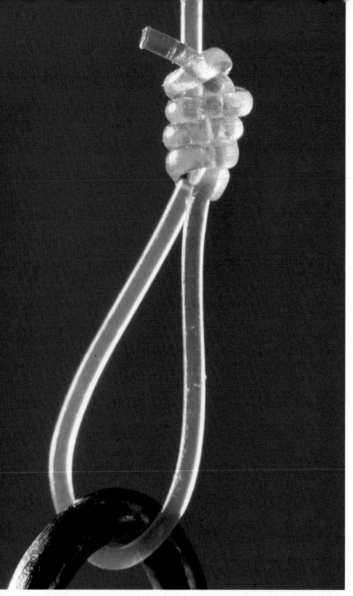

THE DUNCAN LOOP is one of the most versatile fishing knots. It makes an excellent loop knot, and can also be cinched to the attachment eye with a strong pull on the standing line.

# Knots for Use With Artificial Lures

You can improve your success with artificials by learning the best knots for tying on lures, attaching leaders and splicing various types of lines.

Many of the best knots have been shown in previous volumes of The Hunting and Fishing Library, so they will not be repeated here. Some of the strongest knots for tying on lures include the Trilene knot, also called the double clinch; the palomar knot; and the World's Fair knot. These knots all test from 90 to 95 percent of the line strength.

But knots cinched directly to the eye are not the best choice for attaching all lures. With wobbling lures, for example, a knot tightened on the eye may restrict the side-to-side action. A loop knot, such as the Duncan loop, is a better choice in this situation. A knot cinched to the eye may cause a dry fly to become cocked on the leader, making it float unnaturally. A knot that will not allow the fly to swing, like a dry fly clinch, prevents this problem.

When you must use a wire leader, you can keep its visibility to a minimum by attaching the lure with a haywire twist or a twist-melt connection.

For splicing monofilament, most anglers prefer the blood knot. But a blood knot is not the best choice for joining lines and leaders of much different thicknesses or different materials. The triple surgeon's knot, Albright special, nail knot and super glue splice are better choices.

*How to Attach a Lure With a Loop Knot*

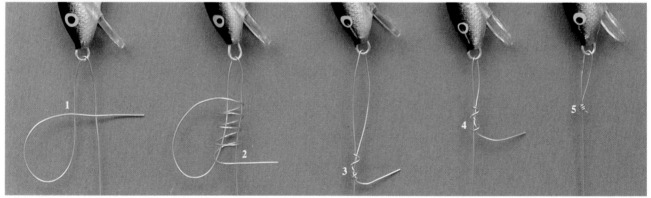

DUNCAN LOOP. (1) Pass the mono through the eye of the lure, then bend it back toward the eye to form a closed loop. (2) Holding the loop and standing line between your thumb and forefinger, wrap the end of the line around the standing line and through the loop four to six times. (3) Start to tighten the knot by holding the lure while pulling alternately on the standing line and tag end. (4) Slide the knot to the desired position by pulling on the standing line. (5) Cinch the knot in place by pulling hard on the tag end with pliers; trim.

## How to Attach a Mono Leader to Braided Dacron or Monofilament Line

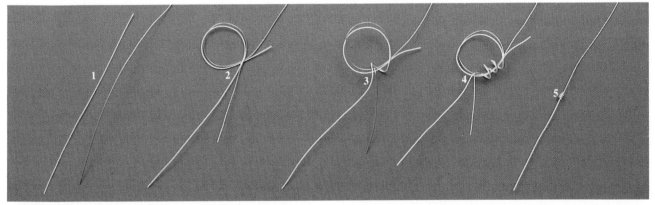

TRIPLE SURGEON'S KNOT. Splice two lengths of monofilament by (1) laying the ends alongside each other so they overlap about four inches. (2) Form a closed loop in the doubled portion of the line. (3) Pass the doubled portion that includes the free end through the loop to form an overhand knot. (4) Pass the doubled portion through the loop two more times. (5) Be sure to moisten the knot, then pull on all four lines to snug it up; trim.

## How to Attach Monofilament to Wire or Heavier Mono

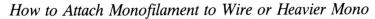

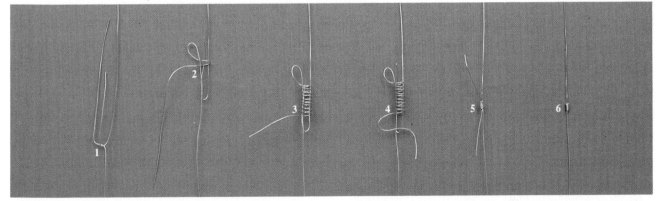

ALBRIGHT SPECIAL. (1) Double the end of a wire or heavy monofilament leader, then pass the standing line through the loop. (2) Hold the standing line against the wire or heavy mono, then wrap the free end around the standing line and leader. (3) Continue wrapping until you complete at least eight wraps, progressing toward the loop. (4) Pass the free end back through the loop. (5) Tighten the knot by alternately pulling on the free end, then on the standing line. (6) Break off the excess wire as you would with a haywire twist (page 14); trim mono.

## How to Attach Fly Line to Leader or Backing

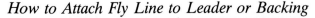

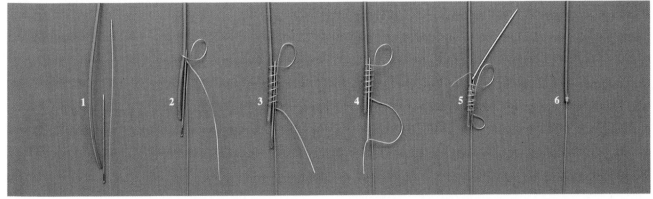

NAIL KNOT. (1) Position a needle alongside the end of the fly line and the butt of the leader. At least 6 inches of the leader butt should extend past the needle. (2) Begin wrapping the butt of the leader around the fly line, needle and standing portion of the leader. (3) Continue wrapping until you complete about five loops. (4) Insert the butt of the leader through the eye of the needle. (5) Holding the loops securely, carefully pull the needle through. (6) Pull on the butt and standing part of the leader to tighten the knot; trim fly line and mono.

## How to Make a Dropper

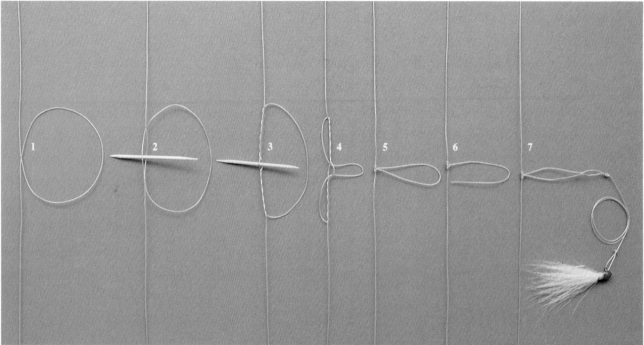

DROPPER LOOP. (1) Make a dropper for attaching an extra lure by first forming a 3-inch loop in the line. (2) Hold the doubled portion of the loop with both hands, then insert a toothpick between the lines. (3) Twist it about four times. (4) Remove the toothpick, then push the loop through the opening where the toothpick was. (5) Tighten the knot by pulling the line on both sides of it. (6) Cut one side of the dropper loop just below the knot to make a single-line dropper, or (7) attach a leader using a loop-to-loop connection.

## How to Attach a Lure to Wire Line

HAYWIRE TWIST. Attach your lure to a single-strand wire leader by (1) forming about three loose twists. Then, (2) make about five tight wraps. (3) Bend the free end into the shape of a handle. (4) Crank the handle several times until the wire breaks off.

TWIST MELT. Attach nylon-coated leader wire by (1) passing it through the eye, then wrapping it around the end of the standing portion five times. (2) Move a lighter back and forth below the twists until the nylon melts together. If you heat it too much, it becomes brittle.

*How to Snell On an Attractor*

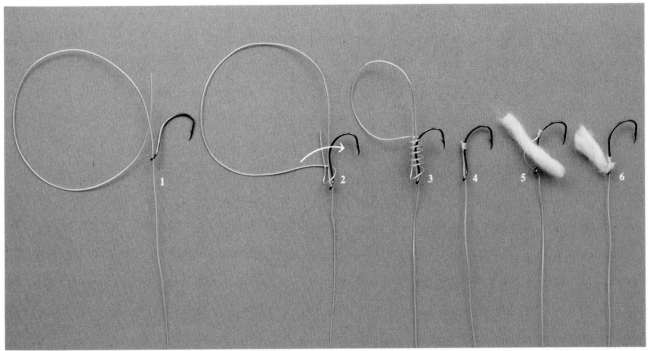

SNELL. Attach yarn or another attractor to your hook by (1) passing about 8 inches of line through the eye and making a loop above the shank. (2) Holding the hook and the loop with one hand, begin wrapping the leg of the loop nearest the eye around the hook, standing line and free end (arrow). (3) Make about five wraps, holding the turns in place with one hand while progressing toward the bend of the hook. (4) Tighten the knot by pulling first the standing line, then the free end; trim. (5) Open the loop; insert yarn. (6) Slide the snell back to the eye.

*Other Knots and Connections*

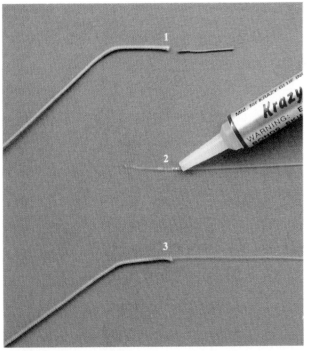

DRY FLY CLINCH. Attach a fly by (1) passing the end of your leader through the eye, then wrapping it around the shank and back out the eye. (2) Wrap the end around the standing line five times. (3) Pass the end between the lines ahead of the fly. (4) Snug up the knot; trim.

SUPER GLUE SPLICE. Attach lead-core line to mono-filament by (1) bending the line back and forth until a ½-inch piece of the lead breaks off. (2) Apply super glue to the mono. (3) Quickly push the mono into the nylon shell from which the lead was removed.

# Leaders, Swivels & Connectors

A leader, swivel or connector that inhibits the action of your lure or appears unnatural to the fish will greatly reduce the number of strikes you get.

When fishing with monofilament, you can usually attach your lure directly to the line. Most other line is too stiff or too visible for direct attachment, so you will need a mono leader. Always use the lightest leader suitable for the type of fish and the conditions. You would need a heavier leader for fishing in timber or brush, for instance, than you would when fishing over a clean bottom.

Many fishermen attach their lures with heavy wire leaders regardless of what kind of fish they expect to catch. But wire leaders are unnecessary and undesirable for most types of freshwater fish.

Fly fishermen should use tapered monofilament leaders. With most flies, a level leader does not have enough momentum to unroll completely on the cast. Tapered leaders may be either knotted or knotless. Knotted leaders consist of several sections of monofilament, decreasing in diameter from butt to tip. Fishermen tailor their own to suit the conditions. Knotless leaders are more expensive, but have no knots to pick up algae. The weight of the *tippet,* or front section of the leader, depends mainly on the size of the fly you are casting. On most spools of tippet material, the weight is designated not only by the breaking strength, in pounds, but also by an X-number. As a general rule, divide the fly size by three to determine which tippet weight to use. For example, a size 18 fly would require a 6X tippet.

Most artificial lures do not require a swivel. A swivel makes the lure appear larger, may change its balance and action, and could increase the chances of tangling on the cast. Without a swivel, however, many lures would twist your line. High quality, ball-bearing swivels generally reduce line twist more than cheap brass swivels.

Some types of artificial lures, such as spoons and vibrating blades, work better when attached with a snap or split ring. Tying your line directly to these lures decreases the amount of action and may cut your line.

A round-nosed snap is a better choice than a V-nosed snap because it allows the lure to swing more freely. Snaps made from a length of continuous wire are generally stronger than the safety-pin type. Select the smallest snap, split ring or swivel suitable for the situation.

*Tips on Using Leaders, Swivels and Connectors*

MAKE a 6-inch *striker* from 20-pound wire line rather than using a commercial wire leader. Attach a swivel and clip with haywire twists (page 14).

SPLICE in a keel swivel 1 to 2 feet ahead of a lure that could severely twist your line. Keel swivels work especially well for trolling.

SOLDER a split ring to greatly increase its strength. Soldering also reduces the chances of the line slipping into the groove and fraying.

16

USE a wire leader only when fishing for northern pike, pickerel or muskies. No other freshwater gamefish have teeth sharp enough to cut through nylon monofilament.

Many experts prefer single-strand wire to multi-strand wire because it is smaller in diameter for its strength and easier to straighten should it become curled.

## Common Mistakes in Attaching Lures

ATTACHING a surface lure with heavy hardware causes the nose to sink. When you twitch the lure, it will not sputter, pop or gurgle.

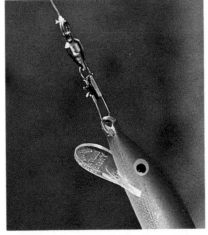

USING a snap-swivel when only a snap is needed may diminish a lure's action. Buy plain snaps or use only the snap from a snap-swivel.

TYING the line in the groove of a split ring rather than on the double wire weakens the connection. And the ring's sharp ends may fray your line.

17

# Downriggers &
# Planing Devices

Trollers often use special devices to run the lures at extreme depths with light tackle or to run lines to the side of the boat.

A *downrigger* has a heavy weight, called a *cannonball* or *bomb*, that attaches to a cable and takes your line deep. When a fish strikes, it trips a release mechanism. This frees the line and enables you to fight the fish with no heavy sinker to detract from the sport.

A *diving plane* uses water resistance instead of weight to carry your lure to the depths. It remains attached to your line. Some models plane sideways at the same time. A strike trips a release, flattening the plane and greatly reducing its resistance so you can reel in the fish without pulling against the plane.

*Side planers* pull your line to the side of the boat. They make it possible to cover more water and to troll lures away from the boat's wake. They work especially well for boat-shy fish like trout and salmon. Side planers can also be used from a stationary boat anchored in current or by an angler on a streambank. The moving water pulls the planer across the stream and keeps the lure working.

Most side planers remain attached to your line. They flatten to reduce water resistance when a fish strikes. A few break loose and float, requiring the angler to go back and get the planer after landing the fish. Others, called *trolling boards,* plane to the side on a cord rather than attach to your line. After the boards are planing, you secure your line to a release, then slide the release down the cord. When a fish strikes, the line breaks free so you can fight the fish without interference from a planer. Trolling boards enable you to fish with multiple lines spaced along the cord's length.

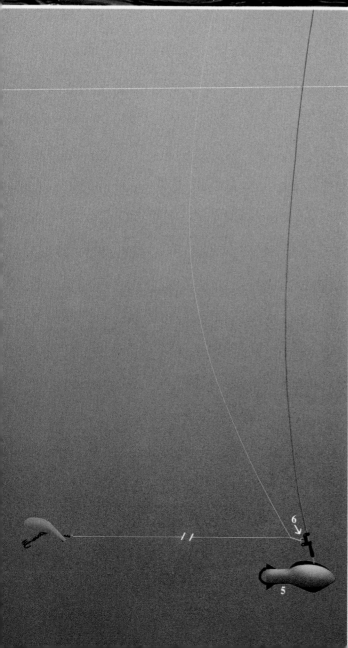

DOWNRIGGERS have a (1) rod holder, (2) large reel filled with light cable, (3) 2- to 4-foot arm to hold the cable away from the boat, (4) brake to stop the (5) 8- to 12-pound weight at the right depth, (6) line release. A (7) counter (downrigger on opposite side) registers the depth.

## How to Use a Downrigger

REEL up the slack after attaching the line to the release and lowering the weight to the right depth. Continue reeling until the rod bows sharply into the set position.

WATCH your rod tip to detect a strike. When a fish grabs the lure, the release mechanism trips, slackening the line momentarily and causing the rod to snap straight.

SET the hook after reeling up the slack line. Another angler should quickly reel up the downrigger weight to prevent the fish from tangling around the cable.

## How to Use Diving Planes

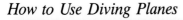

RIG a diving plane by attaching your line to the front eye and a 6- to 8-foot leader to the rear eye. A *rubber snubber* reduces the chance that a fish will break the line when it strikes. Adjust the rudder on a Dipsey Diver® (left); snap the bead (arrow) into the release on a Deep Six® (right).

LET OUT enough line to reach the desired depth. A Dipsey Diver® (inset) will track right, left, or straight, depending on how you adjust the rudder. A Deep Six® will track straight behind the boat.

PLAY the fish carefully. Even though the diving plane flattens when a fish strikes, there is still extra water resistance, so a large fish could snap the line if you exert too much pressure.

## How to Use Trolling Boards

PAY OUT cord with the boat moving ahead. A vertical pole keeps the cord from dragging in the water. Some anglers use a large reel to store the cord and retrieve the board.

ATTACH your line to a release device designed to slide down the cord. To prevent the line from slipping through the release, twist it several times before securing it.

ALLOW the release to slide to within one foot of the board. Engage your reel to stop the line at the right spot. If desired, slide another release halfway down the cord.

## How to Use a Yellow Bird™ Side Planer

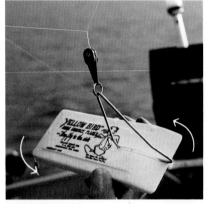

WEDGE your line into the release on the planer after paying out the amount needed. Fishermen sometimes pay out 100 feet or more.

ROTATE the planer to put at least six twists into your line. Otherwise, a fish may pull line through the release, rather than freeing it from the release.

OPEN the snap at the rear of the release and insert your line. The snap keeps the planer attached to the line after a fish strikes.

## How to Use a Hot Shot® Side Planer

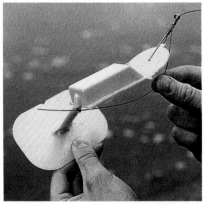

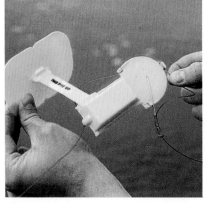

THREAD your line through the front arm, under the body and through the back eye. Tie on your lure and pay out 15 to 30 feet of line.

COCK the arm to the side opposite the rudder, then run the line through the slot on the rudder side and around the front tab four times.

PAY OUT line as the current carries the planer across the stream. A strike will trip the arm so the planer can slide freely on the line.

TROLL with the boards spread at least 40 feet from each side of the boat. In calm or extremely clear water, you may have to spread the boards even farther because these conditions cause fish to move farther to the side of the boat's path.

RETRIEVE the trolling boards and the other lines as quickly as possible when you hook a large fish. If you leave your boards in the water, the fish may swim around one or both of them, wrapping your line on the cord and causing a hopeless tangle.

LET OUT the planer as the boat moves ahead. Like trolling boards, planers should track at least 40 feet to the side of the boat. Stop the planer by engaging the anti-reverse mechanism on your reel.

FIGHT the fish carefully, as you would when using a diving plane. The planer remains attached to your line, sliding all the way down to a split shot (arrow) attached a few feet in front of the lure.

*Other Planing Devices*

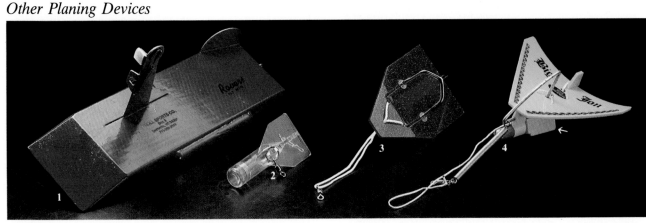

OTHER PLANERS include the (1) Rover, a side planer that detaches from the line when a fish strikes; (2) Jet Planer™, a diving plane that floats at rest; (3) Pink Lady®, a diving plane that flattens when a fish strikes and can be reset by slackening the line; (4) Jonsdiver, a diving plane with a rudder (arrow) that can be adjusted to track right, left or straight. It also flattens when a fish strikes and can be reset by slackening the line.

# Scents

CATCH sunfish in open water or through the ice by attaching a strip of scent-impregnated fabric to a tear-drop jig. The fish cannot tear the fabric off the hook, and the scent will last for hours.

The value of scents in attracting gamefish is a subject that generates much disagreement among fishermen. There is little doubt that species like catfish, sunfish, salmon and trout rely heavily on their sense of smell to find food.

But scent plays a lesser role in the feeding habits of most other gamefish. Predator species like bass, walleyes, northern pike and muskies find food mainly by sight and their lateral line sense, although scent is sometimes a factor.

Fishermen can choose from formulations made of anise or fruit oils; ground-up parts of fish, worms, leeches, crayfish or other popular baits; and even *pheromones,* substances produced by fish that alter the feeding or sexual behavior of other fish.

Most scents come in bottled form and are applied by spraying or pouring them onto the lure. But some soft plastic lures have scent molded in. Some lures have chambers for liquid scent or slowly dissolving pellets that leave a scent trail as the lure is pulled through the water. You can also buy scented fabric that can be cut into strips and pushed onto a hook.

Some manufacturers claim that their product covers up the smell of gasoline or oil. But many fishermen doubt that these odors are offensive to gamefish. In fact, some salmon and steelhead fishermen in the Pacific Northwest believe that lures sprayed with WD-40®, a petroleum-based lubricant, are more effective than untreated lures.

Other manufacturers produce scents intended to mask the smell of *L-serine,* a substance on human skin that repels fish even in extremely low concentrations. But it is questionable if detectable amounts of L-serine remain after a lure has been in the water a few minutes.

Scents may cause a fish to hold onto a lure longer than it otherwise would. For example, bass will actually swallow a soft plastic material with baitfish scent molded in. So the use of scent may, in some cases, give you more time to set the hook.

Fishermen sometimes soak their lures in fish eggs or entrails, ground-up crustaceans and a variety of other natural fish foods. And in many instances, lures tipped with live bait have more scent appeal than those without.

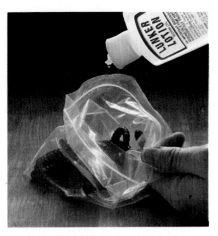

SMEAR scented catfish bait onto a specially designed plastic worm. The substance sticks in the grooves and dissolves slowly. Catfish scouring the bottom detect the scent.

RUB a Vaseline-anise oil mixture on a yarn fly for steelhead and salmon. Melt the Vaseline, then pour in the anise oil. When the mixture cools, apply it liberally to your fly.

PLACE soft plastic lures in a zip-lock bag, then pour in a small amount of oil-based scent. The lures stay clean and soak up the smell, and the oil keeps them pliable.

POPULAR SCENT PRODUCTS include: (1) Gator Bait™, (2) Chena Bait, (3) Whizkers™ Night Crawler Essence, (4) Blakemore Worm Oil, (5) Snagproof Scent Wax, (6) Dr. Juice® Salmon Scent, (7) Stanley Jig and Worm Juice®, (8) Mister Twister Poc'it Potion, (9), Fish Formula II, (10) Bass-X-Citer®, (11) Execution Solution, (12) Lunker Lotion, (13) Mr. Catfish™ Cheese Dip Bait, (14) Catfish Charlie Dough Bait.

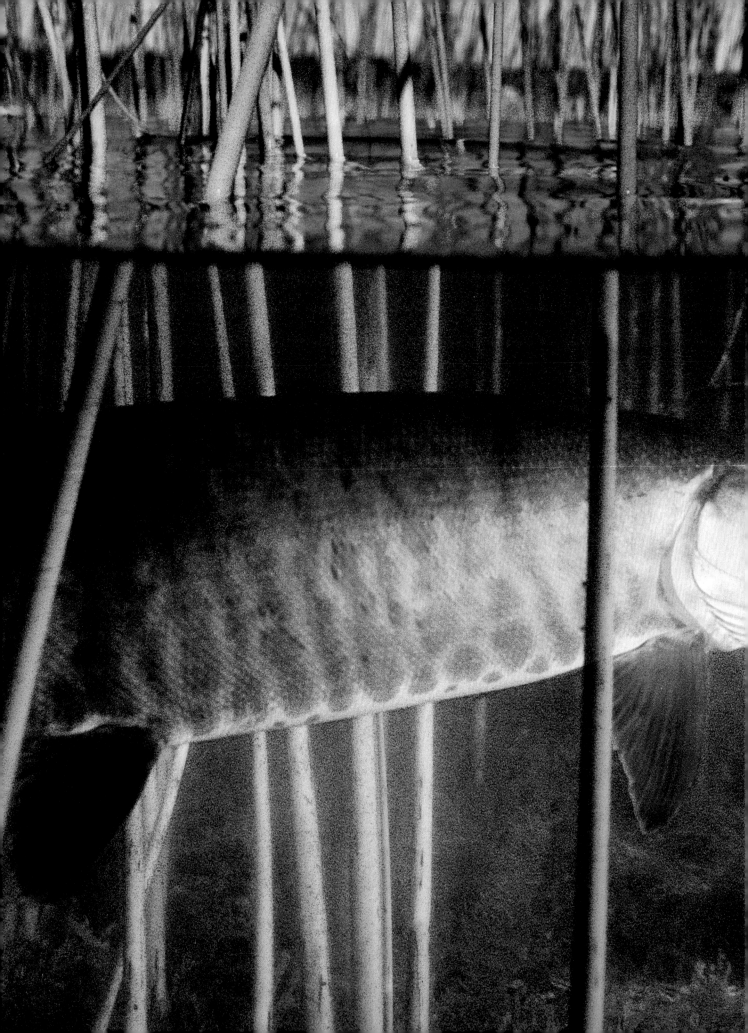

# Spinner-type Lures

# Spinner-type Lures

The dual appeal of spinner-type lures accounts for their success in both clear and murky waters. In clear water, gamefish can spot the flash of the revolving blade from a distance. In murky water, they use their lateral line sense to pinpoint the vibration from the turning blade.

Another reason for the success of these lures is the relative ease of using them. They will produce fish with a simple straight retrieve. And, when a fish strikes a spinner, it often hooks itself.

Spinner-type lures come in four basic designs. Standard spinners have a blade which rotates around a straight wire shaft. Most standard spinners have some type of weight behind the blade to make the lure heavy enough to cast. Weight-forward spinners resemble standard spinners, but the weight is ahead of the blade. Spinnerbaits have a shaft similar to an open safety pin. They have a lead head on the lower arm and a spinner blade on the upper arm. Buzzbaits resemble either standard spinners or spinnerbaits, but have a specially designed propeller rather than an ordinary spinner blade.

Used properly, spinner-type lures will catch almost any kind of freshwater gamefish. These lures will work at any time of year, but are especially effective when extremely cold or warm water makes fish lethargic and reluctant to chase anything moving too fast. Most spinner blades will turn even at very slow retrieve speeds.

Different blades have different amounts of water resistance. A broad blade rotates at a greater angle to the shaft and thus has more resistance than a narrow one. A large blade has more resistance than a small one of the same shape.

The greater the resistance, the shallower the lure will run at a given speed. Generally, wide blades are best suited to slow retrieves and light current; narrow ones to fast retrieves and swift current.

Sensitive tackle will help you feel the beat of the spinner blade. If the beat stops, you may be retrieving too slowly, weeds may have fouled the lure, or a fish may have struck it. When fishing a spinnerbait or buzzbait, use a stiff rod to drive the thick hooks into a fish's jaws.

When fishing spinner-type lures for panfish or trout, use 2- to 6-pound mono; for walleyes or smallmouths in open water, 6- to 10-pound mono; for bass in heavy cover, 12- to 25-pound mono; for casting musky bucktails, 30- to 50-pound braided dacron.

POPULAR BLADES include: (1) Colorado; (2) Indiana; (3) French; (4) willow leaf; (5) fluted, which reflects light in all directions; (6) sonic blade, which spins at a high speed; (7) adjustable scissor-style blade; and (8) buzz blade, which sputters when retrieved on the surface.

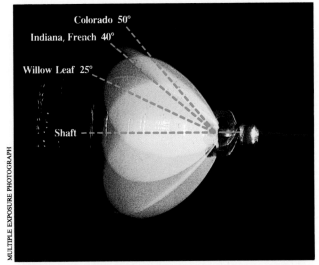

MULTIPLE EXPOSURE PHOTOGRAPH

ANGLE OF ROTATION varies with different styles of blades. Colorado-style blades (above) turn at an angle to the shaft of approximately 50 degrees; Indiana and French blades, about 40 degrees; and willow leaf blades, about 25 degrees.

# Standard Spinners

The standard spinner has gained a world-wide reputation as a top fishing lure. Its simple design has remained basically unchanged for decades.

Because standard spinners sink slowly, they are most effective at shallow or medium depths. They work best in open water, but can also be fished in sparse weeds or over weed tops. They are not as weed-resistant as safety-pin spinners.

Standard spinners come in two main styles. The most common has a blade attached to the shaft with a *clevis*. It produces a strong beat easily detectable by the fish and the fisherman.

A sonic-type spinner has a blade that spins directly on the shaft. The blade is concave on one end and convex on the other. A sonic blade starts rotating at a low retrieve speed. It has less water resistance than a blade mounted on a clevis, making the lure well-suited to fishing in fast current.

Some standard spinners have buoyant bodies made of balsa or low-density plastic. With weight attached to the line, these spinners will float above bottom where they cannot snag on rocks and logs.

Lures shown ½ actual size

POPULAR STANDARD SPINNERS include: (1) Comet®, (2) Rainbo®, (3) Super Vibrax® Salmon' Trout™, (4) Duchess, (5) Cotton Tail®, (6) Rooster Tail®, (7) Purple Ghost Spinner, (8) Minken, (9) Double Cross®, (10) Snagless Sally®, (11) Devil Spinner, (12) J.T. Buel's Fluted Spinner®, (13) Tee-Spoon™, (14) Lightnin'™, (15) Rabbit's Foot™, (16) Duke, (17) Weed Invader, (18) Super Vibrax® Buck™, (19) Buchertail, (20) Harvester TT, (21)

STANDARD SPINNERS come in two basic styles. The (left) clevis type has a blade attached to a *U*-shaped metal clevis that rotates around the shaft. On the (right) sonic type, the shaft runs directly through the blade. The body of a standard spinner is behind the blade and consists of an elongated piece of metal, or of metal or plastic beads. In addition to the body, most spinners also have a separate bead behind the blade to reduce friction.

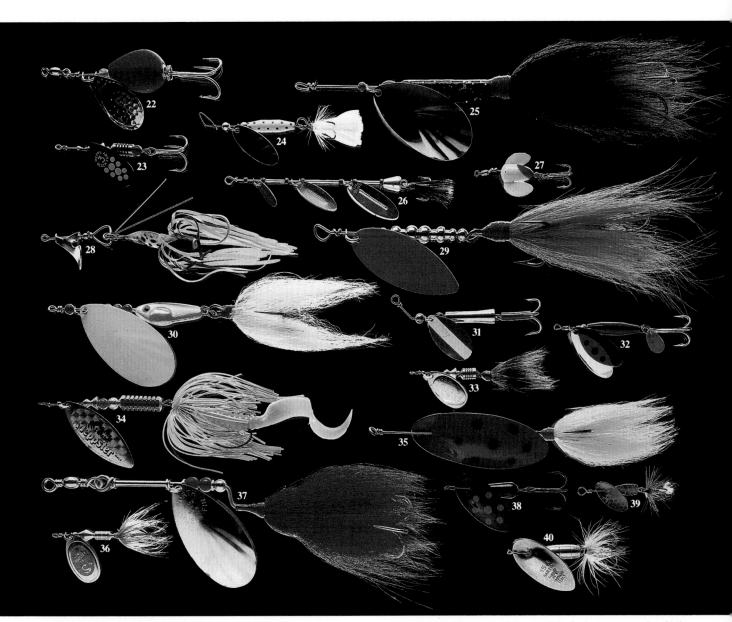

Pike Harasser®, (22) Cherry Bobber®, (23) Black Fury®, (24) Shyster®, (25) Smity Ruslur, (26) Tri-Fly Spinner, (27) Spin-N-Glo®, (28) Hawaiian Wiggler®, (29) Muskie Harasser®, (30) Musky Hot Spot, (31) Notangle® Spinner, (32) Bolo® Spinner, (33) Aglia®, (34) Meppster™, (35) Spotted Marauder, (36) Sonic Rooster Tail®, (37) Musky Fin, (38) Black Panther™, (39) Tiger Tail™, (40) Panther Martin Fly.

# Fishing With Standard Spinners

In a survey conducted by a national muskie fishing club, large bucktail spinners accounted for more trophy muskies than any other lure. Big spinners work equally well for northern pike, and smaller versions excel for pickerel, trout, salmon and smallmouth bass.

When selecting spinners, the main consideration is overall length (from end of shaft to end of hook, including dressing). For small- to medium-sized trout, spinners should measure 1½ to 3 inches; for smallmouth and spotted bass, pickerel, salmon and large trout, 2½ to 4 inches; and for northern pike and muskies, 4 inches or longer.

The blade does not rotate as the lure sinks, so standard spinners generally work better when retrieved steadily than when jigged erratically. In some cases, you may have to twitch the lure to start the blade spinning.

If you reel a spinner at constant speed, fish will often follow without striking. But if you suddenly reel faster, they may grab the lure, thinking it is attempting to escape. Increasing the speed also makes the blade rotate faster, changing the pattern of vibrations and triggering uninterested fish.

When fishing a standard spinner in deep current, you may have to angle your casts upstream to reach the desired depth. If you cast downstream, the blade will spin too fast, giving the lure too much lift.

In shallow current, angle your casts downstream to prevent snagging. Like a thin spoon (page 120), a standard spinner works well when drifted into hard-to-reach spots and allowed to hang in the current.

A major problem in fishing with standard spinners is keeping the blade turning freely. If the clevis becomes bent, it may bind on the shaft, slowing the rotation of the blade. Because standard spinners lack a safety-pin arm or tapered body in front, weeds and bits of algae tend to foul the blade.

Another problem is line twist. The shaft tends to revolve in the direction the blade spins. To minimize twisting, attach the spinner with a ball-bearing swivel. A clevis that is bent or fouled with weeds also causes line twist because water pressure against the fixed blade makes the entire lure spin.

You can also prevent line twist by selecting a spinner with a bent shaft or bending the shaft ahead of the blade so it forms an angle of about 45 degrees. A bent shaft makes a swivel unnecessary.

*Techniques for Fishing With Standard Spinners*

DRIFT-FISH a buoyant spinner for steelhead. Attach a snag-resistant pencil lead sinker about 18 inches ahead of the lure. Cast slightly upstream, then retrieve just fast enough so that the weight maintains contact with bottom. If the lead becomes snagged, a sharp pull will free it from the surgical tubing.

RETRIEVE a standard spinner over submerged weeds to catch northern pike and muskies. To prevent the lure from sinking too deep, raise your rod and begin reeling immediately when the lure hits the water.

## *Tips for Fishing With Standard Spinners*

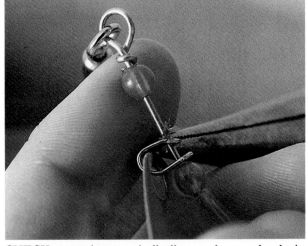

CHECK your spinner periodically to make sure the clevis is not bent, or fouled with bits of vegetation. Straighten a bent clevis with a needlenose pliers.

FIGURE-EIGHT a bucktail spinner at boatside if a muskie or northern pike follows it. Before beginning your figure-eight, push the free-spool button on your reel.

# Weight-forward Spinners

Charter-boat captains on Lake Erie rely almost exclusively on weight-forward spinners to locate walleye schools in the vast expanses of open water. The lures excel whenever fish are scattered over a large area or suspended at a certain depth.

Most weight-forward spinners also work well for fishing in deep water or fast current. They have narrow bodies which cause them to sink rapidly and hold their depth. Others are better suited to shallower water because their wider bodies give them a planing effect. Some models have a long wire shaft in front of the head to reduce the chances of a bite-off when fishing northern pike or muskies.

The lead body on a weight-forward spinner makes it easy to cast. The body is molded to the shaft and acts as a keel, preventing line twist. Because of the position of the weight, the lure sinks head-first. The blade spins while the lure is dropping, attracting fish and tempting them to strike.

Weight-forward spinners are usually tipped with some type of live bait, so most come with a single hook. The hook is attached to ride with the point up, making the lure relatively snagless. Fishermen who use nightcrawlers often replace the single hook with a treble. The worm stays on the hook better and you will lose fewer fish.

POPULAR WEIGHT-FORWARD SPINNERS include: (1) West Sister Twister™; (2) Whizzo®; (3) Lau Lure; (4) Tom's Walleye Lure; (5) Wallbanger™; (6) Front Runner™; (7) Dearie Spinner®; (8) Parrish Lure;

WEIGHT-FORWARD SPINNERS have a lead body molded to the shaft, a spinner blade behind the body and a single or treble hook with or without dressing. Most have a tapered head which slips through weeds.

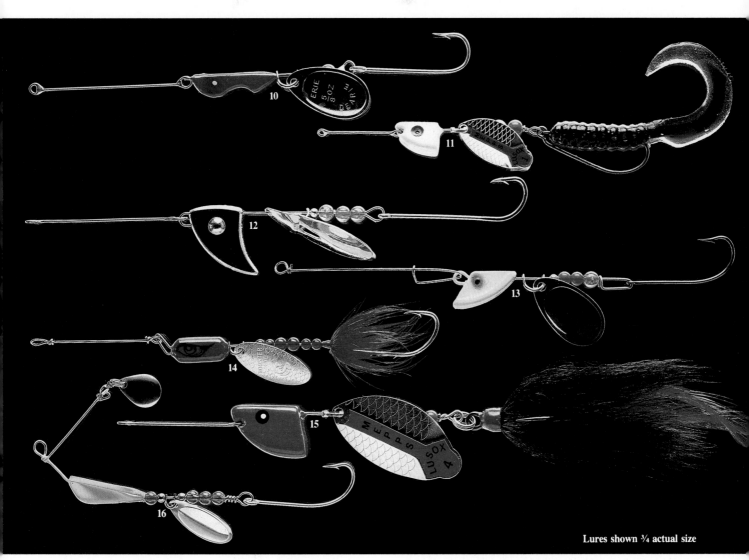

Lures shown ¾ actual size

(9) Paul Bunyan's® "66"; (10) Erie Dearie®; (11) Lusox® Combo Killer, which has a keeper hook to hold a soft plastic tail; (12) Walleye Catcher; (13) Bob Parker's Deep Spin; (14) Rooster Eye; (15) Lusox®; (16) Hot-Spot™.

## Fishing With Weight-forward Spinners

The fast-sinking design makes the weight-forward spinner a natural choice for bottom-hugging fish like walleyes. But these lures will also catch smallmouth and spotted bass, northern pike and trout. Because you can cast them a long distance, weight-forward spinners work well for reaching surface schools of white bass and stripers.

For small- to medium-sized trout, smallmouth and spotted bass, and white bass, use weight-forward spinners from ⅛ to ⅜ ounce; for walleyes and large trout, ¼ to ½ ounce; and for striped bass and northern pike, ½ to 1 ounce.

If cast improperly, weight-forward spinners tangle easily. The lure sails through the air headfirst, so the hook tends to catch on the line. To avoid this problem, use a soft lob cast rather than a snap cast. Stop the lure just before it hits the water. This will turn it around and prevent the hook from catching the line as the lure sinks.

To find the best depth, many fishermen use the countdown technique (page 95). Weight-forward spinners are ideal for this method. They stay at a relatively constant depth when retrieved, so they remain in the fish zone longer than most other lures.

When you begin your retrieve, lift the rod tip sharply to start the blade turning. Begin reeling when you feel the resistance of the blade. Reel fast enough to keep the blade turning.

Weight-forward spinners work well when reeled steadily, but a darting retrieve may produce more fish. Periodically make a long sideways sweep with your rod, then bring your rod forward while reeling rapidly to keep the blade turning. Fish often strike just as the lure begins to accelerate.

Tie a weight-forward spinner directly to your line. Because the lure will not twist your line, you do not need a swivel. A snap or swivel increases the chances of fouling, because the lure can whip around on the cast.

Walleye and trout fishermen often tip weight-forward spinners with nightcrawlers. Pike anglers generally use minnows. Pork rind and soft plastic tails also work well for tipping.

*How to Drift-fish With a Weight-forward Spinner*

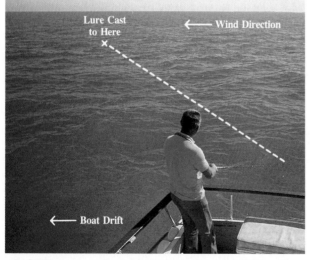

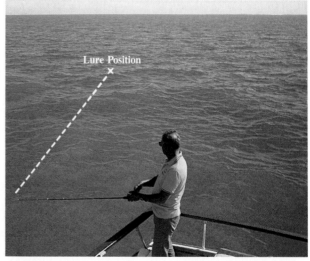

ANGLE your cast downwind as the boat drifts, then count the spinner down to the proper depth. Start your retrieve with your rod on the upwind side, holding your tip low and at an angle to the line.

SWITCH your rod to the downwind side as the lure swings to the upwind side. Keep your rod tip low and at an angle to the line. Holding your rod at an angle increases your sensitivity, so you can detect subtle strikes.

*Tips for Fishing With Weight-forward Spinners*

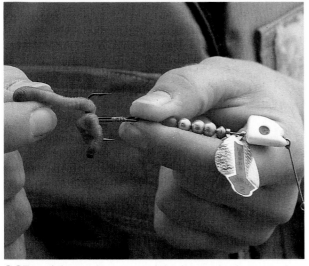

GOB a nightcrawler on a weight-forward spinner so that no more than an inch of the worm trails behind the hook. Crawlers increase the buoyancy of the lure, enabling you to fish slowly just above bottom without snagging.

RIG a soft plastic tail on a keeper hook by (1) inserting the barbed shaft into the tail. (2) Bend the tail before inserting the hook point, then (3) push the hook into the tail until it nearly comes out the opposite side.

SPINNERBAITS include *single blade* models, like: (1) Clearwater Spinnerbait, (2) Spin Dance, (3) CC Spinner, (4) Puddle Jumper®, (5) Mini-Whacker, (6) Falling Star, (7) Hawg Spin™, (8) Chumm'n™ Beetle, (9) Heluva® Spinn, (10) Piggy Boat, (11) Whirlybird, (12) Pomme Special, (13) Bass Harasser®, (14) Tippy, (15) Spin Rig, (16) Lindy Single Spin, (17) Super Rooster Tail®, (18) Hawaiian Eye®, (19) Redman®, (20) Tickle Tail™.

# Spinnerbaits

Spinnerbaits were designed to solve the problems encountered by southern bass anglers in trying to fish reservoirs strewn with timber and brush. Standard or weight-forward spinners snag too easily under these conditions.

The shaft of a spinnerbait is bent in the shape of an open safety pin. The bent shaft prevents weeds and branches from fouling the hook and blade. Yet spinnerbaits hook fish better than most other weedless lures because the entire hook is exposed.

Many fishermen use spinnerbaits to locate fish in shallow water. You can cover a lot of water quickly and the flash and vibration draw strikes from the most aggressive fish. Even if a fish does not take the lure, it may follow and reveal its location. Then, you can use a slower or less flashy lure to catch it.

When selecting spinnerbaits, consider the length of the upper arm, the thickness of the shaft and the shape of the head.

In most situations, use a spinnerbait with an upper arm long enough so that the blade rides above the hook point. Models with a shorter arm work best for helicoptering (page 39). But if the arm is too short, it will not protect the hook from snags or provide enough stability to keep the lure from rolling. If the arm is too long, it will reduce your hooking percentage because fish often strike at the blade.

A thin-wire shaft transfers the vibration from the blade to the skirt for maximum wiggle. And thin wire enables you to hook fish more easily because it collapses on the strike. A thick-wire shaft is better in timber and brush because it deflects off branches.

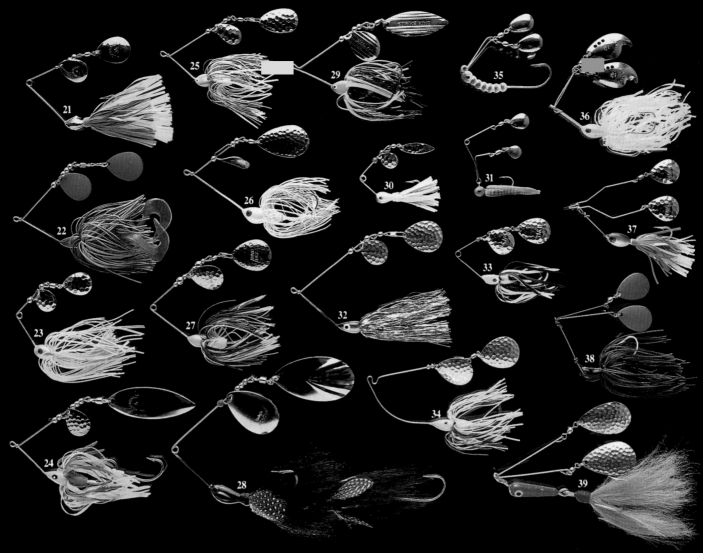

Lures shown ⅜ actual size

*Tandem blade* models include: (21) Pro Gold™, (22) Rub-Grub™, (23) H & H Spinner Bait, (24) Big Bass™, (25) Weed Wader, (26) Roto Spin, (27) Buzz Bullet™, (28) Musky Tandem, (29) Strike King Spence Model, (30) The Joker, (31) Mr. Mean®, (32) Tinsel Tail™, (33) Slot Back, (34) Switch Blade. *Twin blade* models include: (35) D'Crawler, (36) Maxi Twin Spinner, (37) Bushwhacker Twin (38) Go-For-It, (39) Musky Twin.

Most spinnerbaits have a pointed or bullet-shaped lead head molded to the lower shaft. The streamlined head helps the lure snake through weeds. Some small spinnerbaits have a detachable free-swinging jig instead of a fixed head. The jig is not as weedless, but hooks fish better.

Spinnerbaits come in single-blade, tandem-blade and twin-blade models. Single-blade types produce the strongest beat, and helicopter well, making them a good all-around choice. Tandems have more water resistance, so they run shallower at a given retrieve speed and are effective for bulging the surface (page 38). Twin-blade types are best in heavy cover because the dual upper shafts protect the hook better than a single shaft.

Most spinnerbaits have skirts of vinyl, live rubber, bucktail, tinsel, mylar or marabou. But some, called spin-rigs, come without skirts and are intended for use with live bait or pork strips.

SPINNERBAITS include the (1) single spin, which has a single blade attached to the end of the upper arm with a barrel or snap-swivel; (2) tandem spin, which is similar to a single spin, but has another blade on a clevis on the upper shaft; (3) twin spin, which has two separate upper shafts, each with a single blade.

BULGE the surface with a spinnerbait by holding your rod tip high and reeling just fast enough so the blades do not quite break the surface. Bulging works best in warm water when fish feed actively in the shallows.

## Fishing With Spinnerbaits

Many professional bass anglers rely heavily on spinnerbaits for fishing the varied waters encountered on the tournament circuit. The spinnerbait's versatility makes it a good choice for a broad range of fishing situations.

A spinnerbait can be fished with many different retrieves. You can reel slowly along bottom, at moderate speed a few feet below the surface, or fast enough so the lure bulges or breaks the surface. You can also hop a spinnerbait along bottom or jig it vertically around cover. Crappie fishermen even troll with spinnerbaits when searching for fish in open water. Experiment with different retrieves to find the one that is best for the conditions.

A properly-tuned spinnerbait does not twist when retrieved, so you should tie it directly to your line. A snap or swivel will increase the chances of the lure tangling in the line.

If your spinnerbait has a coil of wire for an eye, your line may pass between the arms and wedge in the coil. If this happens, cut the line and retie to eliminate the frayed mono. Spinnerbaits with an open slot for an eye will not catch the line.

Fishermen often fail to recognize strikes when using spinnerbaits. Fish commonly strike with only a gentle nudge. Whenever you detect a pause in the beat of the blade, set the hook.

Spinnerbaits often work better when tipped with a pork strip or live bait, particularly nightcrawlers and minnows. Some panfish anglers remove the soft plastic grub tails and substitute live grubs, worms, bits of shrimp or pieces of scent-impregnated fabric.

While spinnerbaits were designed primarily for catching largemouth bass, they also work well for smallmouth and spotted bass, crappies, sunfish, northern pike, pickerel and muskies. Spinnerbaits weighing $\frac{1}{32}$ to $\frac{1}{8}$ ounce work best for panfish, $\frac{1}{8}$ to $\frac{3}{8}$ ounce for smallmouth and spotted bass, $\frac{1}{4}$ to 1 ounce for largemouths and pickerel and up to 3 ounces for large muskies and northerns.

HELICOPTER a spinnerbait alongside vertical cover like a submerged tree. Keep your line taut to detect any change in the beat. Helicoptering works best in cold water or when sunlight drives fish into deep cover.

CAST a spinnerbait beyond an obstruction like a stump, then retrieve so that the lure bumps the cover. The momentary break in blade rotation often triggers a strike. The shady side of the cover is usually most productive.

## Tips for Using Spinnerbaits

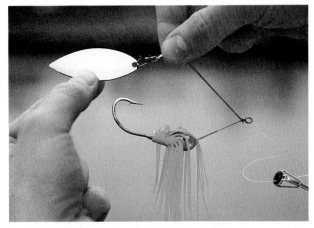

ASSEMBLE your own spinnerbaits from components. You can buy plain arms and add blades and lead-head jigs. Or, you can buy arms with the heads molded on, then add blades, swivels and skirts.

REPLACE the standard Colorado blade on your spinnerbait with a much larger willow-leaf blade. The willow-leaf blade has more flash and can be retrieved more rapidly, so it works better for locating active fish.

SHORTEN the upper arm to make a spinnerbait helicopter better. For best performance, the blade should ride ahead of the hook. To make the lure drop more slowly, use a larger blade.

ATTACH a stinger hook by sliding a small piece of rubber tubing over the end, then pushing the spinnerbait hook through the eye. The rubber keeps the stinger in line with the arms for protection from snags.

# Buzzbaits

A hungry bass in the shallows finds it difficult to resist the splash and sputter of a buzzbait. Few other lures create as much surface disturbance.

All buzzbaits have a double- or triple-winged propeller, called a *buzzblade*, rather than an ordinary spinner blade. On some buzzbaits, the blade turns on a safety-pin shaft identical to that of a spinnerbait. On others, it turns on a straight shaft like that of a standard spinner.

The buzzblade is designed to operate half in and half out of the water, resulting in the gurgling surface action. Some buzzbaits have counter-rotating twin blades for even more disturbance.

Because the buzzbait is designed solely for surface fishing, it is not as versatile as the spinnerbait. But a buzzbait often works better than a spinnerbait for fishing over shallow, weedy flats. The buzzblade is less likely to foul in weeds or grass than an ordinary spinner blade. A buzzbait may also work better than a spinnerbait in murky water. Even when fish cannot see the lure, they can hear the sound of the blade breaking water.

Buzzbaits work best in relatively calm water. If there is too much wave action, fish do not seem to notice the surface disturbance from the lure.

Some fishermen tip their buzzbaits with plastic worms or pork strips for extra action. These attractors also add buoyancy so the lure stays on the surface. But if the attractor trails too far behind the hook, fish will often strike short.

BUZZBAITS include *safety-pin* models, like: (1) Clacker, (2) Triple Wing®, (3) Buzz King, (4) Pistol Pete, (5) Rocker Buzz™, (6) Weed Eater, (7) Chatter Buzz, (8) Pro Buzz 3, (9) T's Shaker, (10) Paddle Whacker, (11)

BUZZBAITS include: (left) safety-pin type with a buzz-blade that rotates around the upper arm and (right) straight type with a buzzblade that turns on the main shaft and a weedless hook. Both types may have double blades that rotate in opposite directions. Most buzzbaits come with skirts of plastic, live rubber or bucktail.

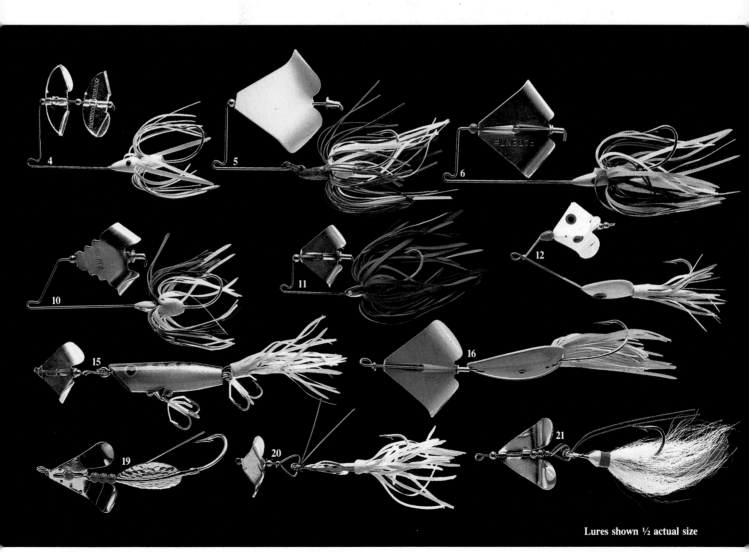

Lures shown ½ actual size

Turbo, (12) DD III®. *In-line* models include: (13) Hobo, (14) Floyd's Buzzer™, (15) Sputterbuzz®, (16) Lundahl Buzz Spoon, (17) Musky Hawk, (18) Herb's Dilly™, (19) Skitter-Buzz, (20) Sputterfuss®, (21) Uncle Buck's™.

## Fishing With Buzzbaits

Buzzbaits have gained a reputation as one of the best shallow-water lures for largemouth bass. But many fishermen do not realize that these lures also work well for northern pike, pickerel and muskies.

For largemouth bass and pickerel, use buzzbaits from ¼ to ⅝ ounce; for northern pike and muskies, from ⅝ to 1 ounce.

When fishing for bass, reel a buzzbait steadily, just fast enough to keep it on the surface. For pike, muskies and pickerel, a faster retrieve is usually more productive. Fishing in slop usually requires a slower retrieve than fishing in open water or sparse vegetation. Dense overhead weeds make it difficult for a fish to zero in on a fast-moving lure.

When a slow retrieve is needed, select a twin-bladed buzzbait or one with a wide, spoon-type body. The twin blades give the lure more lift, and the flattened body keeps it planing on the surface. The choice of safety-pin versus in-line styles depends mostly on personal preference.

To keep your lure on the surface, stop it just before it hits the water. This removes the slack from your line

*How to Make a Tandem Buzzbait Veer to the Side*

REMOVE the counter-rotating blades (above) from *two* buzzbaits by sliding off the stops. Reassemble the two lures so that both blades turn in the same direction (below). One altered lure will veer right, the other left.

WALK the lure that veers right into hard-to-reach places on your right-hand side. Use the other lure for cover on your left. This technique works especially well for fishing under docks or overhanging limbs.

MULTIPLE EXPOSURE PHOTOGRAPH

so you can start your retrieve before the lure has a chance to sink. While retrieving, hold your rod tip high enough so that your lure stays on the surface, but not so high that you cannot set the hook.

Fish are sometimes difficult to hook with buzzbaits. Because of the dense cover, they may have trouble catching the lure. They splash or swirl nearby but miss the hook. If you jerk too soon, you will pull the lure away. Instead, wait until you see or feel the fish grab the lure before you set the hook.

To improve your chances of hooking fish, add a stinger. Rig a long-shaft single hook so the point rides up and secure it exactly the same way as rec-ommended for spinnerbaits (page 39). In open water, use a treble hook for the stinger.

Buzzbaits work especially well in spring, when largemouths are spawning on shallow, weedy flats. Cast beyond a nest, then reel the lure directly over it. Later in the season, buzzbaits work best on calm mornings or evenings, on overcast days or at night, the times when most predator fish prowl weedy or brushy shallows.

Do not hesitate to cast a buzzbait into the thickest, most impenetrable cover, especially in hot weather. Few lures are more effective for drawing fish from beneath the slop.

*Other Tips for Fishing With Buzzbaits*

TUNE your buzzbait on the way to the lake by ex-perimenting with different ways of bending the blade, then holding the lure out the car window. When the blade spins fastest, the lure is properly tuned.

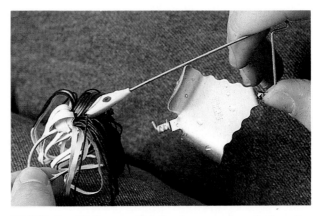

BEND the blade arm slightly downward so that as the blade rotates, it just ticks the shaft. The extra noise may attract more fish, especially at night. Avoid bending the arm so much that the blade cannot turn rapidly.

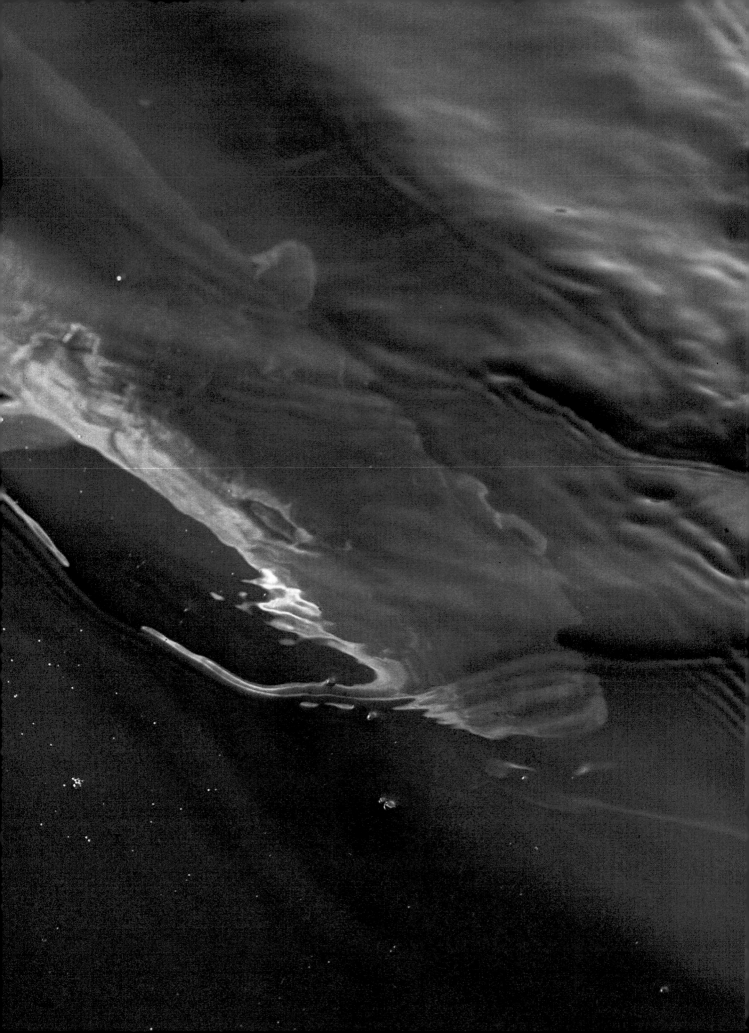

Plugs

# Plugs

Originally, the term *plug* referred to a lure carved from a block of wood. Many fishermen still consider wooden plugs the best, but most modern plugs are made of hollow plastic or hard foamed plastic.

Plastic plugs are less expensive and hold their finish better than wooden plugs. Plastic plugs of a given model are more consistent in shape, density and action than wooden ones. But wooden plugs sometimes have a better action than similar ones made of plastic. A balsa minnow, for example, wobbles more readily than a plastic minnow of the same size and shape.

Most plugs imitate baitfish, but some resemble animals like mice, frogs and crayfish. Other plugs attract fish by their action and flash, resembling nothing in particular. All plugs produce some sound that draws the attention of gamefish. It may be a high- or low-frequency vibration; a pop, gurgle or splash; or merely the sound of the hooks clinking on the hook hangers. A few plugs have chambers filled with shot that produce a loud rattle.

Some plugs are designed exclusively for surface fishing. Surface plugs work especially well when fish are spawning or feeding in shallow water. But they will sometimes draw fish up from deeper water.

Surface plugs are most effective at water temperatures of 60°F or warmer. The water must be relatively calm; otherwise, fish do not seem to notice the action. Surface plugs generally work best in early morning, at dusk or at night, although they may catch fish any time of day. They fall into the following categories:

*Stickbait* — These long, slender, floating plugs lack lips or propellers. They have no built-in wobble, so the fisherman must supply the action.

*Propbait* — Similar to stickbaits, these lures have a propeller at one or both ends.

*Crawler* — A large face plate or wings on the sides make the lure crawl across the surface when retrieved steadily. Crawlers produce a plopping or gurgling sound.

*Chugger* — The indented face catches water when the plug is jerked across the surface, producing a popping or chugging noise. Some chuggers have a slow, swimming action when retrieved steadily.

Subsurface plugs run at depths of 1 to 20 feet, and with added weight can be fished much deeper. These plugs are much more versatile than surface plugs. They work well in either calm or rough water and will catch fish at any time of day. You can select either shallow- or deep-running models, depending on the depth of the fish. Subsurface plugs fall into these categories:

*Crankbait* — Most crankbaits float at rest, but some sink. All have a lip which makes them dive and wiggle when retrieved.

*Minnow plug* — Like crankbaits, these plugs have lips and may float or sink. Designed to imitate thin-bodied baitfish, minnow plugs have an attractive side-to-side wobble.

*Vibrating plug* — These thin-bodied plugs do not have lips. The attachment eye is on top of the head, resulting in a tight wiggle. Most vibrating plugs sink, but a few float while at rest.

*Trolling plug* — Designed primarily or exclusively for trolling, these plugs generally have a large flattened forehead that creates a wide, erratic wobble. Trolling plugs are difficult to cast because they are relatively light, and their shape is too wind resistant. Most trolling plugs float at rest.

*Jerkbait* — These large, elongated plugs are intended mainly for catching muskies and large pike. Most float at rest, dive when given a strong jerk, then float back to the surface. Many have metal tails that can be bent to change the action.

Plugs range in size from the tiny, inch-long models used for panfish to the huge, foot-long plugs intended for muskies. When selecting plugs, length is a more important consideration than weight. Following are plug lengths most commonly used for various types of gamefish.

| SPECIES | PLUG LENGTH |
|---|---|
| Crappies | 1 to 2 inches |
| Small to medium trout | 1 to 3 inches |
| White bass | 1½ to 3 inches |
| Smallmouth and spotted bass | 2 to 3 inches |
| Largemouth bass and pickerel | 2 to 6 inches |
| Walleyes | 3 to 6 inches |
| Salmon and large trout | 3 to 7 inches |
| Northern pike, muskies and stripers | 4 to 12 inches |

# Stickbaits

A stickbait walked noisily across the surface will draw gamefish from deep water better than any other surface lure. In clear water, fish may rush the lure from 15 feet down.

Stickbaits rank among the top lures for big largemouths, but they also work well for smallmouth and spotted bass, white and striped bass, pickerel, northern pike and muskies.

The basic stickbait retrieve is called *walking-the-dog*. Because of the way it is balanced, a stickbait will move in an alternating left-right-left manner

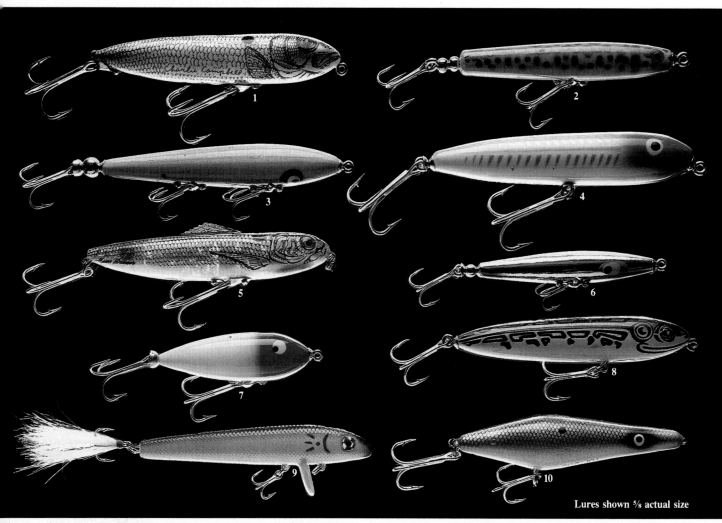

POPULAR STICKBAITS include: (1) Original Signature Zara Spook®; (2) Bomber Stick Bait; (3) Devil's Warhorse®; (4) Ol' Line Sides; (5) Mann-Dancer, with internal beads that produce extra noise; (6) Devil's Toothpick; (7) Baby Zara Spook®; (8) Dog Walker; (9) Walkin' Stick®, which also has internal beads. The lip on the bottom adds side-to-side motion; (10) Top Dog, made of tough, flexible foam.

when retrieved with short, sharp jerks. This action mimics a crippled minnow struggling on the surface.

With a little practice, you can walk a stickbait to one side, enabling you to reach cover to the right or left of your retrieve path.

Fish often bulge or swirl the surface near a stickbait without grabbing the lure. Wait until you actually feel a tug before setting the hook.

A fast-action rod with a springy tip works best for walking-the-dog because it enables you to twitch the lure sharply. Stickbaits work best when fished with relatively light line, usually from 8- to 10-pound test. Light line allows the lure to move from side to side easily. Like other surface lures, stickbaits should be tied directly to the line, without snaps or leaders. For pike or muskies, use a wire leader no heavier than necessary to hold the fish.

STICKBAITS consist of a long body, usually tapered at each end, with extra weight (arrow) at the rear. The attachment eye is at the nose.

*How to Walk-the-Dog*

CAST a stickbait over submerged weeds or brush, then give it a sharp twitch (left), letting your line go slack while the lure skids to one side. As soon as the lure stops, twitch again (right) and let the line go slack while the lure skids

in the other direction. Continue twitching to make the lure walk in a zigzag fashion. To walk the lure to one side, make jerks in rapid succession rather than waiting for the lure to stop between jerks.

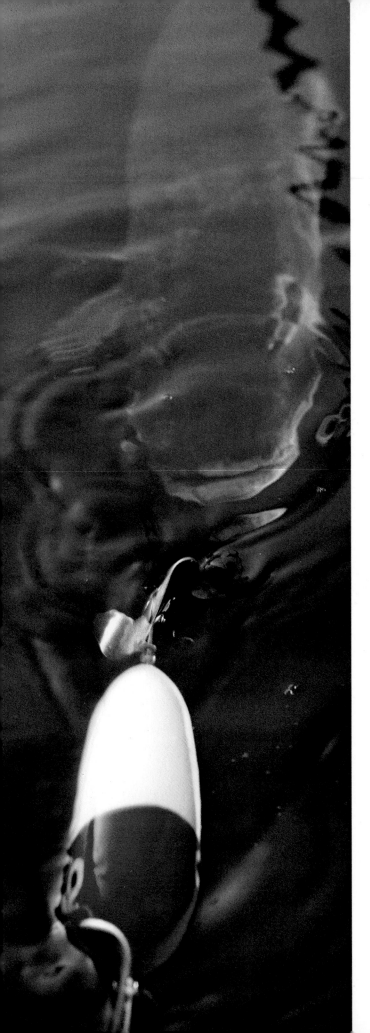

# Propbaits

Propbaits are the most versatile of all surface lures. You can fish small spots thoroughly with a twitching retrieve or cover large areas by reeling rapidly. And propbaits create more disturbance than most other surface lures, so they work well even when wind ripples the surface.

A slow, twitching retrieve generally works best for largemouth, smallmouth and spotted bass; a fast, steady retrieve for pike, muskies, stripers and white bass. A few propbaits have a weight in the rear, so they can be fished with a walk-the-dog retrieve.

Some propbaits have a flattened or dished face, resulting in a more erratic action than models with a pointed nose. Models with a propeller on each end create the most disturbance and work best for fast retrieves. On some brands, the twin props counter-rotate to prevent the entire lure from spinning.

The tackle used with propbaits is similar to that used with stickbaits. And like stickbaits, propbaits are usually tied directly to the line. If you use a heavy snap and leader, the nose may run below the surface, preventing the propellers from throwing water.

PROPBAITS have an elongated, usually unweighted body, and an attachment eye at the nose. Some models have a propeller at only one end, others have propellers at both ends.

PROPBAITS include: (1) Dalton® Special, (2) Boy Howdy®, (3) Hardworm® Top Water, (4) Hellraiser, (5) Spinner Minnow, (6) Dying Flutter™, (7) A.C. Shiner 203, (8) Jerk 'N Sam, (9) Cisco Kid Topper, (10) Tiny Torpedo®, (11) Devil's Horse®, (12) Bomber Popper, (13) Bass Agitator, (14) Creek Chub® Injured Minnow, (15) Snake Bait, (16) Nip-I-Diddee®, (17) Spin Scout, (18) Trophy, (19) Skipjack, (20) Topper Stopper™, (21) Mud Puppy.

## *Tips for Fishing With Propbaits*

TUNE the blades if they do not spin rapidly. Adjust the angle by bending the blades backward or forward (above); the pitch by twisting them.

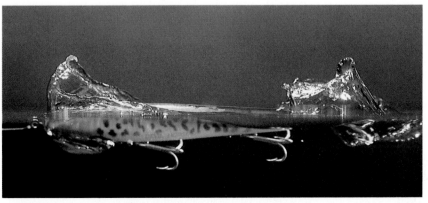

TWITCH a propbait with slack line for the best action. By starting with slack line, you can jerk the lure more sharply than you could with a taut line, yet the lure will move only a few inches. Continue retrieving in short twitches followed by pauses until the lure pulls away from the cover.

# Crawlers

Crawlers excel when exploring for fish in large expanses of shallow water. They work best with a steady, moderately fast retrieve, enabling you to cover a lot of area quickly.

Many largemouth bass fishermen rate crawlers among the best lures for night fishing. The continuous plopping sound makes it easy to monitor the lure's location. And with a steady retrieve, the line stays taut so you can detect strikes. Crawlers also work well for northern pike, pickerel and muskies.

Models with a face-plate will swim through sparse weeds without fouling. But hinged-arm models tend to collect bits of weeds or algae at the arm joints.

The speed at which you retrieve a crawler is critical. Too fast, and the plug will skim the surface with little action. Too slow, and it will not produce the gurgling sound. The best speed is that which produces the most pronounced wobble and the loudest gurgle.

If fish do not strike with a steady retrieve, try adding an occasional pause and twitch. Or, stop reeling periodically and let the ripples subside.

CRAWLERS have either (1) a wide cupped face plate or (2) arms, which are usually collapsible, on the sides of the body. All crawlers have relatively stocky bodies and attachment eyes at the front. The force of water alternately pushing on one side of the face or one arm, then the other, produces the wide wobble.

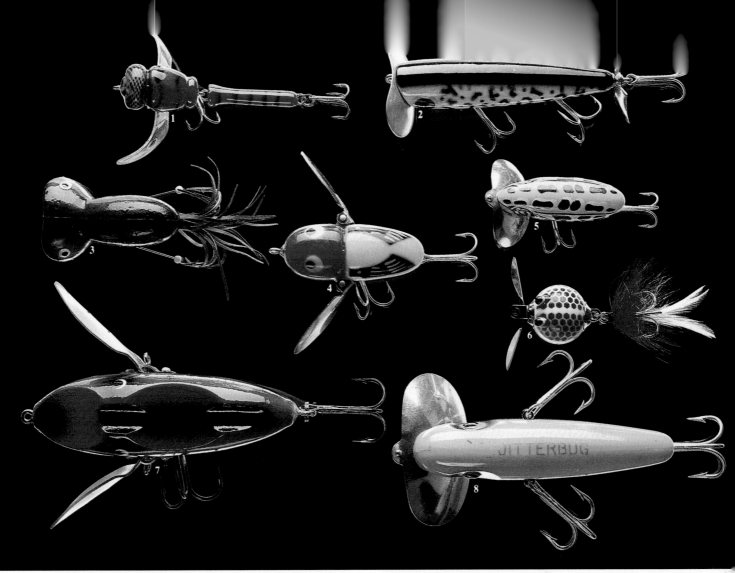

POPULAR CRAWLERS include: (1) Tombo; (2) Dalton Twist®; (3) Bassassin, made of flexible plastic; (4) Crazy Crawler®; (5) Jitterbug®; (6) Flutter-Fin; (7) The Creeper; (8) Musky Jitterbug®.

## *How to Make Crawlers More Weedless*

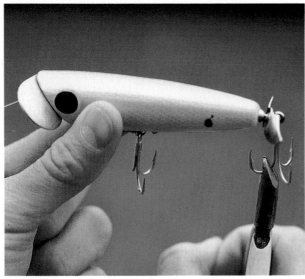

POSITION the treble hooks so that only one point of each hook aims forward, then cut off the front points. The hooks ride with points up and slide easily over weeds.

SECURE the side trebles on a Musky Jitterbug® above the body with a rubber band, wire or heavy monofilament. Or, remove the side trebles from the lure.

# Chuggers

A chugger could be described as an overgrown fly-rod popper. Like poppers used for fly-fishing, chuggers have a scooped-out, grooved or flattened face that makes a popping or chugging sound when the lure is twitched.

Generally considered largemouth bass lures, chuggers will also catch smallmouth and spotted bass, as well as schooling stripers. They are not as effective as other surface lures for pike and muskies.

Chuggers work better than most other surface lures for fishing precise targets. To fish a small opening in a bed of lily pads, for example, cast a chugger into the spot and wait for the ripples to die. Often, fish will strike almost immediately. If not, give the lure a twitch, moving it forward only an inch or so. Then wait for the ripples to die again. If nothing strikes after two or three twitches, cast to another opening.

How hard you twitch a chugger depends on the mood of the fish. Jerking too hard creates an explosion of water, causing the fish to spook. A moderate twitch usually works better; and, at times, fish prefer a gentle twitch that barely disturbs the surface.

Fishing small pockets is more difficult with a chugger than with a fly-rod popper. With fly-fishing tackle, you can place the lure more accurately and lift it off the water without catching weeds. To make a chugger more weedless, trim the front point of each treble (page 53).

Pinpoint casting is important when using a chugger. A slow- or medium-action rod enables you to cast more accurately than a fast-action rod. In dense-cover situations, use line from 12- to 20-pound test. Otherwise, 8- to 10-pound line is adequate.

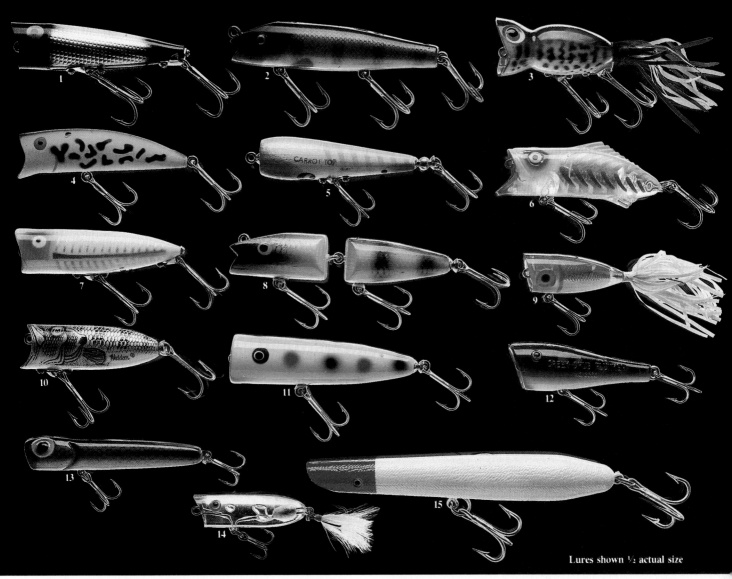

Lures shown ½ actual size

POPULAR CHUGGERS include: (1) Pico® Pop, (2) Creek Chub Darter, (3) Hula Popper®, (4) Bomber Popper, (5) Carrot Top, (6) Throbber, (7) Chugger Spook®, (8) Sam's Jointed Chub, (9) Trouble Maker, (10) Lucky 13®, (11) Pop'n Sam, (12) Creek Chub Plunker, (13) Chug Bug®, (14) Near Nuthin'®, (15) Pencil Popper®.

## Tips for Fishing With Chuggers

TIE a small jig to the rear hook of a chugger to catch white bass, stripers or other surface schooling fish. The chugger provides casting weight and creates a surface disturbance, increasing the effectiveness of the jig.

MULTIPLE EXPOSURE PHOTOGRAPH

WORK a grooved-face chugger beneath the surface to imitate a frightened minnow. Point your rod at the lure, and reel until the head dips under water. Then, jerk repeatedly while reeling to give the lure a darting action.

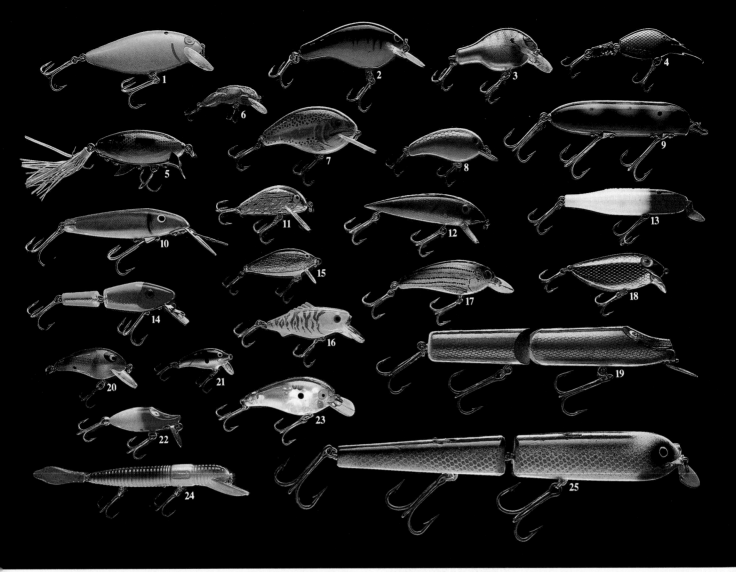

CRANKBAITS include *shallow to medium runners,* like: (1) Speed Shad®, (2) Kill'r "B" 3, (3) Small Fry Bream, (4) Sparkle Tail®, (5) Spence Scout, (6) Teeny Wee-Crawfish™, (7) Mini-R®, (8) Big O®, (9) Bass Oreno®, (10) Cisco Kid, (11) Quarterback®, (12) Maverick, (13) Creek Chub Pikie, (14) Jointed Mirrolure®, (15) A.C. Shiner 200, (16) Shad-Mann, (17) Model A®, (18) ThinFin® Silver Shad®, (19) Scamper Jointed, (20) Bo-Jack, (21) Mini Fat Rap®, (22) River Runt Spook®, (23) Little L, (24) Hardworm®, (25) Jointed Smity. *Deep divers* include:

# Crankbaits

Fishermen use the term *crankbait* for any lure with a lip that causes it to dive and wiggle when cranked in. Designed primarily for casting, most crankbaits have a relatively short aerodynamic body. Minnow plugs are sometimes classed as crankbaits, but will be considered as a separate category in this book.

Crankbaits work best at water temperatures of 55°F or warmer. At cooler temperatures, fish usually refuse to chase fast-moving lures.

Because you can cast a crankbait a long distance and retrieve it rapidly, you can cover a lot of water quickly. Even when fish are not actively feeding, the intense wiggle often triggers strikes. And when fish are feeding, more will see your plug than would see a lure that moves more slowly.

Most crankbaits float at rest, but a few sink, enabling you to count them down to the desired depth before beginning your retrieve.

Crankbaits are made of foamed or hard plastic or wood, usually balsa or cedar. Hard plastic crankbaits generally cast better than foamed plastic or wooden ones of a similar design, but do not wiggle as well on a slow retrieve.

The type of lip determines how deep a crankbait will dive. Many fishermen believe that a crankbait with a steeply-sloping lip dives the deepest. But in reality, one with a lip extending straight off the front runs deeper. The size of the lip in comparison to the body also affects the running depth. The longer and wider the lip, the deeper the lure will dive. Crankbaits with small, steeply-sloping lips may run as shallow as 3 feet; those with large, straight lips, as deep as 12 feet. Some deep divers will reach depths of 25 feet when trolled on a long line.

(26) Hi-Contrast™, (27) Fastrac Shad™, (28) Mud-Bug®, (29) ThinFin® Hot 'N Tot®, (30) Double Deep Shad™, (31) Bomber®, (32) Wally Diver™, (33) Lunker Licker, (34) Super-Dawg, (35) Snipe, (36) Diving Bang-O-B, (37) A.C. Shiner 301, (38) Shadling®, (39) Deep Little "N", (40) Diving Kill'r "B" 2, (41) Stinger, (42) Rooter, (43) Arbo-Gaster®, (44) Water Dog, (45) Shad Rap™, (46) Natural Ike™, (47) Deep-Digger, (48) Deep Pig Razorback®, (49) Deep Running Fat Rap®, (50) Wiggle Wart®, (51) Hellbender.

Shallow-running crankbaits work best for fishing on shallow flats or over submerged weeds or brush. Deep divers would dig into the bottom or foul quickly under these circumstances. But deep divers are better suited for fishing deep structure, like a sharply-sloping shoreline. For extremely deep water, use a sinking crankbait.

Some crankbaits have metal lips which can be bent to make the lure run deeper or shallower. But the majority of crankbaits have fixed lips that cannot be adjusted. Most fishermen carry a selection of crankbaits with different types of lips, so they can fish at different depths.

The lip on a crankbait serves another important purpose. Most crankbaits run in a head-down position, so the lip contacts obstructions before the hooks do. As a result, the lure usually deflects off solid objects such as rocks and logs before the hooks can become snagged.

CRANKBAITS include (top) shallow runners with small, steeply-sloping lips and attachment eyes at the nose and (bottom) deep divers with large, straight lips and attachment eyes on the lip.

# Fishing With Crankbaits

Some fishermen argue that crankbait fishing is boring because all you have to do is cast out and reel in. But anyone who has shared a boat with an expert crankbait fisherman knows better.

You must select a crankbait that runs at the proper depth. To determine how deep a crankbait tracks, retrieve the lure through water of a known depth, feeling for it to touch bottom. If it does, move to slightly deeper water and try again. Continue until the lure no longer touches, then note the depth.

Many fishermen believe that the faster you retrieve a crankbait, the deeper it will dive. Actually, every crankbait has an optimum speed at which it performs best. Too slow, and it will not dive or wiggle properly. Too fast, and it will turn sideways and lose depth. Experiment with different retrieves to find the speed at which the lure tracks the deepest.

A crankbait will not attain maximum depth unless tuned so that it tracks perfectly straight. Depending on the type of lip, a crankbait must be tuned by bending or twisting the eye, bending the lip itself, or bending the attachment wire.

Experienced crankbait fishermen sometimes mistune their crankbaits intentionally to make them run to the side. By mistuning your plug, you can fish beneath overhead cover like a dock, or bump your plug into vertical cover like a seawall.

To reach maximum depth with a crankbait, cast as far as possible and keep your rod tip low while retrieving. With a shorter cast or higher rod position, you will begin pulling the plug upward before it reaches its potential depth.

Line diameter also affects how deep your crankbait runs. Thin line has less water resistance and allows the plug to run deeper than thick line. The smaller the plug, the more it is affected by line diameter.

When fishing a crankbait in open water or light cover, 6- to 12-pound mono is usually adequate. But you may need mono up to 25-pound test for fishing in heavy cover. Spinning tackle works well for shallow-running plugs or deep divers that do not pull too hard. But bait-casting tackle is better for deep-diving plugs that have a lot of water resistance.

For the best action, tie a crankbait directly to your line. If the plug does not have a split ring on the eye, use a Duncan loop (page 12). A heavy leader or snap-swivel will restrict the plug's wobble.

To keep your lure in the fish zone as long as possible, cast parallel to the structure or cover. For example, to work the shady side of a log, cast parallel to the log and retrieve the lure along its length. If you cast perpendicular to the log, your lure would be in the fish zone only a fraction of the time.

The way you retrieve a crankbait depends on the water temperature and the mood of the fish. In cool water or when fish are reluctant to strike, a stop-and-go retrieve usually works best. Fish often strike when you stop reeling and the lure starts to float upward. In warm water or when fish are actively feeding, a fast, steady retrieve is most effective.

When a fish grabs a crankbait it often hooks itself. But strikes can be much more subtle. If the fish hits while moving in the same direction as the lure, you will feel only a slight slackening of the line. Set the hook whenever you feel a change in the action.

Crankbaits will catch practically any type of gamefish except the smallest panfish species. Mini-crankbaits, measuring only about one inch in length, work well for good-sized panfish.

## *How to Tune Different Crankbaits*

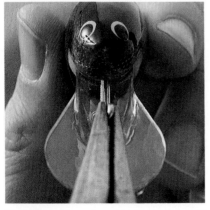

BEND or turn the attachment eye if the plug tracks to the side. If the plug tracks to the left, bend the eye to the right and vice versa.

TUNE a crankbait with a wire connecting arm by bending the wire in the same direction you would bend the eye on an ordinary crankbait.

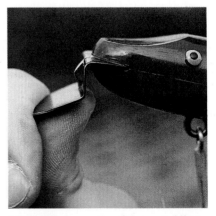

ADJUST the angle of the metal lip to change the running depth. Bending the lip down makes the lure run shallower but wiggle more.

RIP a crankbait through broadleaf weeds to catch pike, muskies or bass. The interruption in the plug's action often triggers a strike. Or, bounce the plug off a stump or other obstruction.

## Techniques for Fishing With Crankbaits

BUMP a crankbait along bottom by continuing to reel rapidly even after feeling bottom contact. The combination of noise, erratic action and stirred-up bottom debris often draws strikes from uninterested fish.

MULTIPLE EXPOSURE PHOTOGRAPH

UNSNAG a floating, deep-diving crankbait by letting the line go slack if the lure catches in timber. The lure will float upward and backward, freeing itself. Some anglers remove the front treble to make the lure more snag-free.

59

# Minnow Plugs

Minnow plugs have a shape and swimming action remarkably similar to those of shiners or other slim-bodied baitfish.

Because minnow plugs rely mainly on their visual appeal to attract fish, they work best in relatively clear water. They do not produce as much sound as crankbaits or vibrating plugs, so they are less effective in waters of low clarity.

Minnow plugs generally have smaller lips than crankbaits, so the head does not swing as far to the side when the plug swims. The tight rocking action is less violent than the action of a crankbait, but much more lifelike.

Originally, minnow plugs were hand-carved from balsa wood. Many are still made of balsa, but some are now molded from plastic. Because of their light weight, balsa models wobble more than plastic ones. But they are harder to cast and less durable.

Most minnow plugs float at rest, but some sink. The majority of floaters run shallow, from 1 to 5 feet below the surface, although some have very long lips and dive as deep as 12 feet.

Floating minnow plugs rank among the top lures for casting or trolling along shallow shorelines, over shallow reefs or above the tops of submerged weeds. They can also be twitched erratically across the surface. Floaters work extremely well at night. Fish can easily see the silhouette of the shallow-running plug against the surface. Sinking models can be counted down to any depth, but they have less wobbling action than floaters.

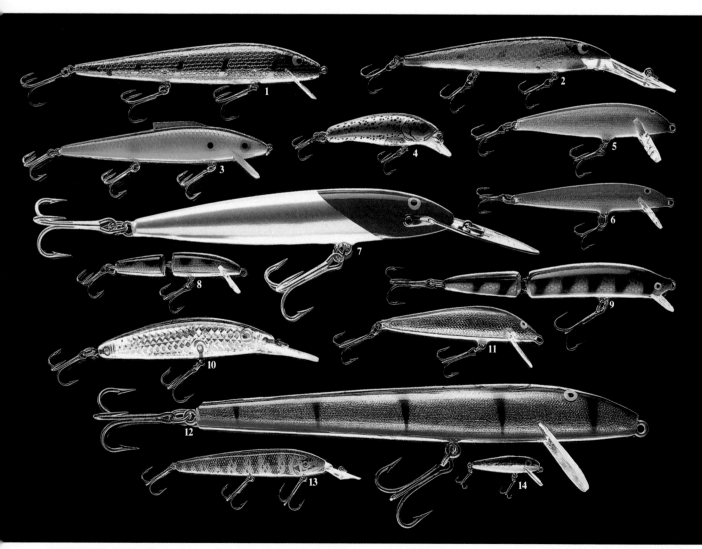

MINNOW PLUGS include: (1) Rattlin' Rouge, (2) Spoonbill Deep Diving Rouge, (3) Rat-L-Stik, (4) Mini Long A®, (5) CountDown™ Rapala®, (6) Original Floating Rapala®, (7) Magnum CountDown™ Rapala®, (8) Jointed Floating Rapala®, (9) Jointed Nilsmaster®, (10) Variant®, (11) A.C. Shiner 375, (12) A.C. Shiner 1000,

MINNOW PLUGS include (left) balsa and (right) plastic models. Both have attachment eyes on the nose, and plastic or metal lips. Many balsa plugs (cross-section) have an internal wire connecting the attachment eye to the hooks. The wire insures that the hooks will not pull out of the soft wood, allowing the fish to escape.

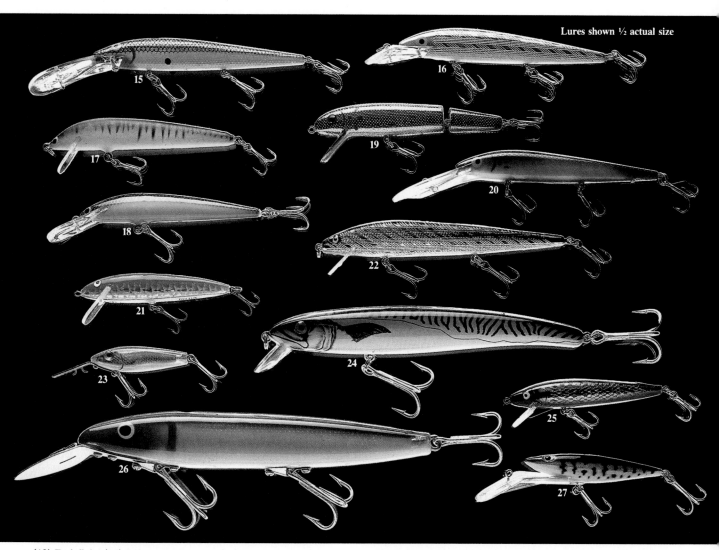

Lures shown ½ actual size

(13) Baitfish, (14) Minnow/Floater, (15) Spoonbill™ Minnow/Floater, (16) Fastrac™ Minnow/Floater, (17) Bang-O-Lure, (18) Diving Bang-O-Lure, (19) Jointed Red Fin®, (20) Deep Diving Red Fin®, (21) Palsa, (22) Rip-N Minnow®, (23) L&S Shiner Minnow, (24) Long A® Magnum, (25) Hellcat, (26) Husky Cisco Kid, (27) Arby®.

# Fishing With Minnow Plugs

The effectiveness of minnow plugs is not surprising because most gamefish prefer thin-bodied baitfish to those with deeper bodies. Baitfish with slim bodies are easier to swallow and less likely to lodge in a predator's throat.

Minnow plugs appeal to almost all gamefish, with the exception of small panfish. They work best for largemouth, smallmouth and spotted bass; walleyes; northern pike, muskies and pickerel; stripers and trout.

If you attach a minnow plug improperly, you will dampen its wiggle, making it less effective. A loop knot or small, round-nosed snap works best. Before casting, check the hooks to make sure that they are hanging straight. If they are cocked in the hook hangers, the plug will not run true.

Because of their light weight, floating minnow plugs are difficult to cast. For maximum casting distance, use spinning tackle and the lightest line practical for the conditions. Light line also allows the lure to wiggle more freely. Bait-casting tackle can be used with the larger sinking minnow plugs.

When casting a floating minnow plug in the shallows, use the wind to your advantage for maximum distance. When trolling in shallow water, let out a lot of line, up to 150 feet. Long-distance casting and long-line trolling reduce the chances of fish spooking when they see you or your boat. Unlike most crankbaits, floating minnow plugs will continue to run shallow despite the long length of line, so they are less likely to foul.

To work a floating minnow on the surface, cast it into a likely spot, then retrieve it with sharp twitches. Pause a few seconds after each twitch, as you would when fishing with a popper or chugger.

You can fish a sinking minnow plug on bottom by allowing it to sink until the line goes slack before beginning your retrieve. Reel just fast enough so that the lure bumps bottom occasionally. For suspended fish, count down a sinking minnow plug to the proper depth, just as you would count down a jig (page 95).

In most situations where a sinking minnow plug works well, a floating minnow plug will work even better. Attach a bottom-walker or pinch-on sinker ahead of the plug to reach the desired depth. The floating plug has a more attractive action and is less likely to snag because it rides farther off bottom.

Some fishermen doctor their floating minnow plugs to make them neutrally buoyant. A standard floating minnow plug must be retrieved at moderate speed to prevent it from rising quickly to the surface. A neutrally buoyant plug can be retrieved much more slowly, yet it will maintain its depth. Slower retrieves often work better in cool water or when fish are sluggish.

*How to Make a Minnow Plug Neutrally Buoyant*

SLIP a mono noose over the plug, then pinch on enough shot so the lure barely sinks in a tub of water. Move the noose to find the balance point.

DRILL a hole large enough for the shot just below the center line and directly in line with the position of the noose.

CENTER the shot in the hole; otherwise the plug will tip to one side in the water. Seal both ends of the hole with epoxy glue.

*Tips for Fishing With Minnow Plugs*

BEND the attachment eye to change the action of a minnow plug. Bend the eye downward for more wiggle; upward for less.

COAT damaged areas on the surface of a balsa minnow plug with fingernail polish. Otherwise, the wood will soak up water, ruining the plug's action.

CHANGE the silver finish on a minnow plug to another color with an indelible marking pen. The finish will retain its reflective quality.

# Vibrating Plugs

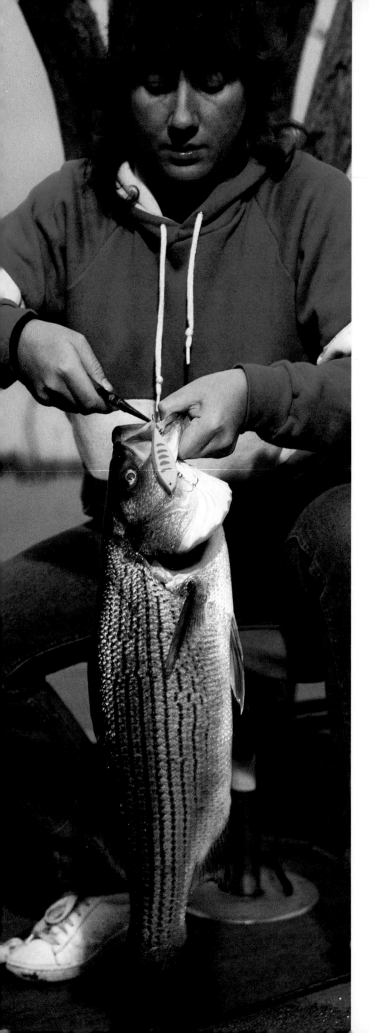

The tight wiggle of a vibrating plug creates high-frequency sound waves that attract fish even in cool or murky water. Vibrating plugs work best for large-mouth, smallmouth and spotted bass; northern pike; walleyes; white bass and stripers.

Because most vibrating plugs sink rapidly, they are more versatile than crankbaits. Without changing lures, you can retrieve along bottom in deep water, count down to suspended fish, or start retrieving immediately after the cast to catch fish near the surface. Vibrating plugs work well with a steady retrieve, but a darting retrieve varies the frequency of the vibrations and may trigger more strikes.

Vibrating plugs lack lips, so they are not as snag resistant as crankbaits. They work well in open water or along the edges of weeds, brush or timber. But they snag easily in dense cover.

A vibrating plug is ideal for covering a lot of water quickly. The narrow body has little wind or water resistance, so you can cast long distances and retrieve rapidly. The shot pellets in models with rattle chambers increase casting distance even more.

For maximum wiggle, attach a vibrating plug with a loop knot, never with a heavy leader or snap-swivel. A sensitive graphite or boron rod helps detect changes in the vibration that could signal a strike or indicate that the plug has become fouled.

VIBRATING PLUGS have an attachment eye on the back, causing the plug to run with its head angled down. Water pressure on the forehead produces the tight vibrating action. Vibrating plugs do not have lips.

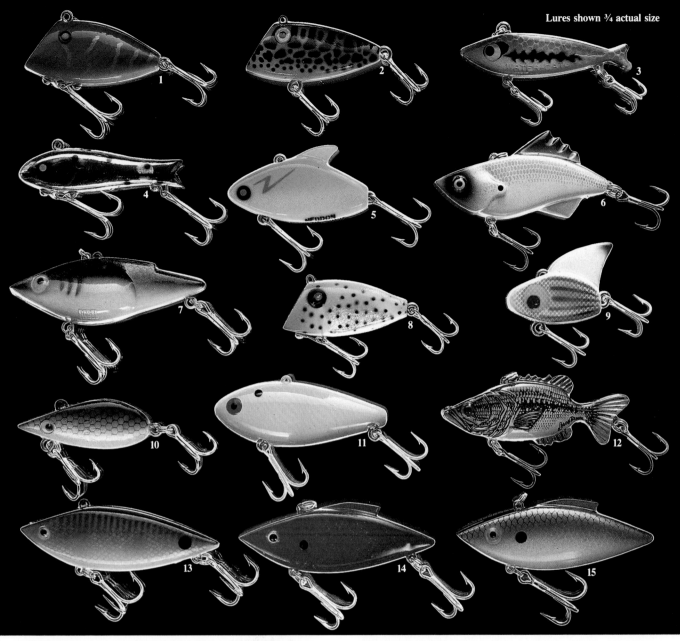

POPULAR VIBRATING PLUGS include: (1) Swimmin Minnow, (2) Bayou Boogie, (3) Water Gater, (4) Speck Minnow, (5) Super Sonic®, (6) Finn Mann®, (7) Racket Shad®, (8) Pico® Chico, (9) Sail Shark, (10) Whiz Bang®, (11) Pinfish, (12) Leroy Brown, (13) Th'Spot®, (14) Rat-L-Trap, (15) Floatin' Rat-L-Trap.

## Tips for Fishing With Vibrating Plugs

MULTIPLE EXPOSURE PHOTOGRAPH

USE a vibrating plug that floats for fishing around shallow cover or for surface-schooling fish. Retrieve with your rod tip low, alternately reeling to draw the lure under the surface, then pausing so it floats back up.

FREE a snagged plug with a specially-designed aluminum pole. Place your line inside the wire pigtail (inset). Then, with the line tight, slide the pole down until the pigtail hits the plug.

# Trolling Plugs

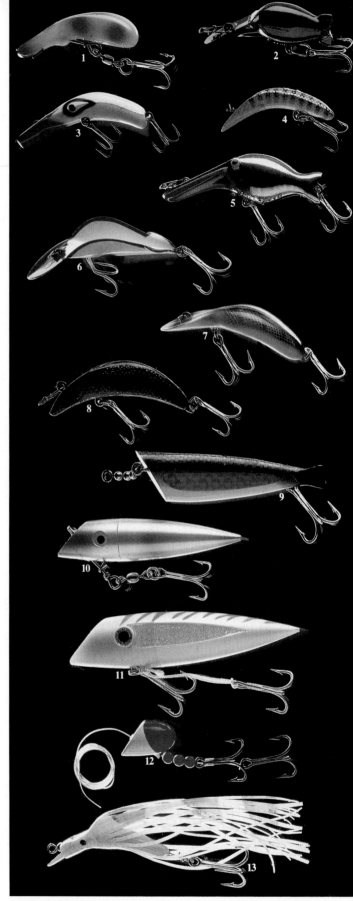

Trolling plugs differ greatly in appearance and action, but share one common feature: their design makes them difficult to cast. Many have too much wind resistance, some tangle too easily and others are simply too heavy.

Most trolling plugs have broad, flat foreheads that produce an exceptionally wide wobble. Some have lips or scooped-out heads that give them a narrower, crankbait-like wobble. A few have flattened faces, resulting in an erratic, darting action.

Fishermen generally use trolling plugs to cover large open-water areas. Trolling plugs are not suited for working a target precisely because it is difficult to control their path unless trolling with a short line.

When selecting trolling plugs, consider the depth at which they run and the speed at which they have the best action.

If the fish are located within 20 feet of the surface, you can choose a trolling plug that runs at the proper depth with no added weight. The best way to determine exactly how deep a plug will run is to test it yourself. Few plugs run deeper than 20 feet, so you will need sinkers, downriggers or diving planes to reach fish below that depth.

The speed and action fish prefer change from season to season and sometimes even from day to day. For consistent success, your plug selection must change accordingly. Experienced trollers generally carry a selection that includes speed-trolling plugs, which attain their best action at speeds from 5 to 7 mph; slow-trolling plugs, which reach peak performance at only 1 to 2 mph; and plugs which operate best at intermediate speeds.

TROLLING PLUGS include: (1) Fire Plug®; (2) Hot Shot®; (3) Lazy Ike®; (4) Flatfish; (5) Macadoo™; (6) Spoonplug®; (7) Tadpolly®; (8) Fishback®; (9) Cutplug®; (10) Canadian Plug® (11) Tiger Plug™; (12) Wobble Troll;

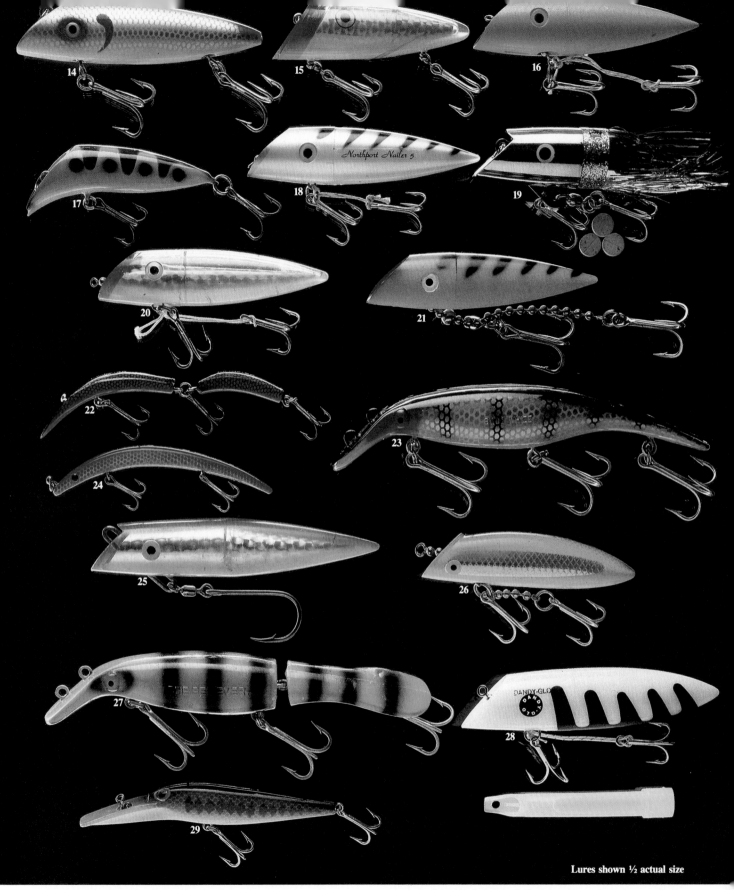

Lures shown ½ actual size

(13) Shakey Pete™; (14) Spar X; (15) Mac's Squid™; (16) J-Plug®; (17) Canadian Wiggler; (18) Northport Nailer; (19) Pop-Tail™, which has a hollow head for holding scent-releasing pellets; (20) Silver Horde; (21) Lucky Louie®; (22) Kwikfish®; (23) Swim Whizz; (24) Dorado®; (25) Tomic; (26) Witch Doctor®; (27) Believer™; (28) Dandy-Glo™, which has a hollow body for holding a Cyalume® lightstick; (29) Little Mac™.

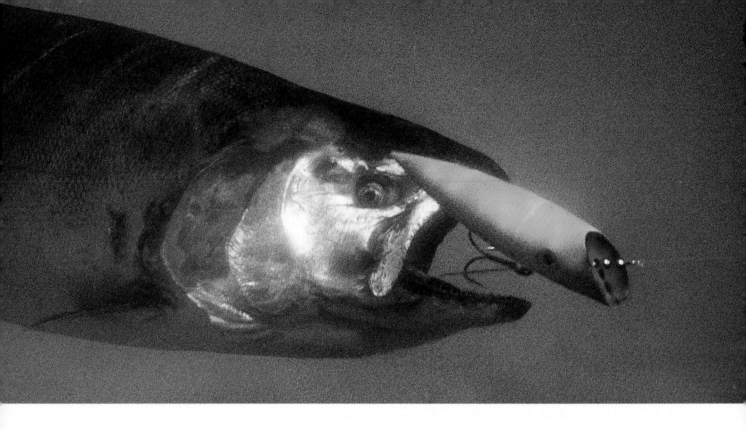

## Fishing With Trolling Plugs

Trolling with plugs may not be the most exciting fishing method ever devised, but it is certainly one of the deadliest. Trolling is the best technique for exploring open water and enables you to keep your plug at a selected depth indefinitely.

Because they work best in open water, trolling plugs are most effective for salmon, trout and striped bass. When fished along edges of cover, like weed-lines, trolling plugs will also take walleyes, bass, northern pike and muskies.

If you simply let out your line and motor about at random, you stand little chance of catching fish. Plan your trolling route so that your plug seldom strays away from likely cover, structure or a precise temperature layer.

Fishermen use a wide variety of electronic aids to help them catch fish with trolling plugs. Flashers and graph recorders are invaluable for determining the proper depth. Try fishing at different levels and note the depth immediately when you hook a fish. Chances are there will be more fish at the same level.

A water temperature gauge helps locate fish, like salmon and trout, that have very specific water temperature preferences. You will greatly improve your odds of catching fish by keeping your lure in the preferred temperature layer.

Trolling speed indicators help you keep your plug moving at the speed that produces the best action.

Downrigger fishermen sometimes use sophisticated water temperature-trolling speed monitors that provide readings at the depth the lures are running. Readings taken at the depth of the lures are more meaningful than surface readings. Temperatures at a particular depth often change dramatically as you troll. And currents on the surface may differ greatly from those in the depths, giving you a false idea of how fast your lure is moving.

Many anglers make the mistake of trolling too far off bottom in an effort to avoid snags. Unless fish are suspended in a specific temperature layer, you will usually draw more strikes by trolling deep enough to make your plug dig sand or bounce off rocks.

Another common mistake is trolling at the same speed regardless of the plug. Different plugs run best at different speeds, and the only sure way to find the best speed is to experiment. When using multiple lines, remember to use plugs designed to run at the same speed.

Multiple lines enable you to compare different actions, colors and sizes. If one plug begins to produce, attach similar plugs to all the other lines.

Trolling rods should be stiff enough to withstand the strong pull of the plug, but they need not be sensitive. Downrigger rods should be at least 7½ feet long and flexible enough to bend into the set position. Speed-trolling rods should be very stiff and no more than 5½ feet long. Level-wind reels are a better choice than spinning reels for most trolling situations. They minimize line twist and make it easier to return your plug to the right depth.

## How to Use a Water Temperature-Trolling Speed Monitor

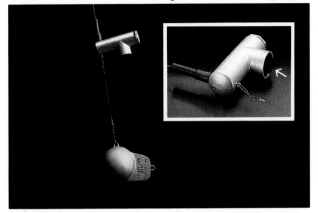

LOWER your cannonball to the desired depth with the sensor (inset) on the cable. The front face of the sensor measures temperature and the impeller (arrow) measures lure speed at the depth you are fishing.

WATCH the meter closely when trolling. If the water temperature changes, adjust your fishing depth to find the right temperature. You may have to speed up or slow down your motor to maintain a constant lure speed.

## Other Ways to Maintain the Proper Trolling Speed

TIE a 6-foot piece of line to the back of the boat and attach a *pilot plug* identical to the one you are using. Watch the action of the pilot plug to determine if you are trolling at the right speed.

CHECK your speed with an electric trolling speed indicator. The meter measures the rate at which water passes by an impeller on the underside of the boat, registering the exact speed to the nearest ¹⁄₁₀ mile per hour.

## How to Return Your Plug to the Right Depth

NOTE the color when you hook a fish while using metered line, then let out to that color again. Most metered lines change color every 10 yards.

MARK your line with a waterproof pen when your plug is at the proper depth. Then, stop at the same mark when you let the plug out again.

COUNT the number of times the level-wind passes back and forth when letting out line. Use the same number of passes the next time.

# Jerkbaits

A jerkbait imitates a large baitfish in distress, diving below the surface, then floating back up or darting erratically from side to side. The term *jerkbait* results from the sharp, jerky retrieve needed to give the plug its action. Jerkbaits have practically no action with a steady retrieve.

Nearly all jerkbaits are made of wood. They fall into two categories: high-buoyancy models, most of which have a metal tail to make them dive; and low-buoyancy models, which do not have tails. High-buoyancy models stop quickly after being jerked, then rise rapidly to the surface. Low-buoyancy models have more side-to-side action, glide forward after the jerk, and rise to the surface more slowly.

Most jerkbaits dive from 2 to 4 feet, although some go as deep as 8 feet. Because the density of wood varies greatly, one jerkbait may dive or glide differently than another of the same model.

Jerkbaits will catch fish throughout most of the open-water season. If the water temperature is below 60° F, use a low-buoyancy jerkbait and work it slowly. In warmer water, use either style of jerkbait and work it more rapidly.

When you give a jerkbait a sharp pull, it displaces a large volume of water as it darts ahead. Fish sense the sound and vibration, so they will strike jerkbaits in either clear or murky water.

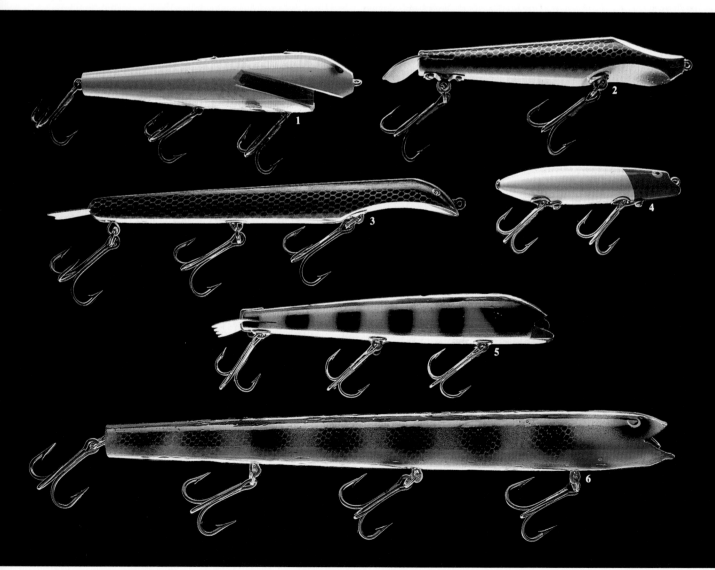

POPULAR JERKBAITS include *high-buoyancy* models, like: (1) Reef Hawg™; (2) Junior Fooler; (3) Suick Muskie Thriller; (4) Bomber Jerk Bait; (5) Bobbie Bait; (6) Smity Custom Jerk Bait. *Low-buoyancy* models in-

JERKBAITS include (top) high-buoyancy models which have a fluke-like metal tail and/or a grooved head to make them dive, and (bottom) low-buoyancy models which usually have internal lead weights and no tails. Most jerkbaits have an attachment eye near the tip of the nose and 2 or 3 extra-strong treble hooks.

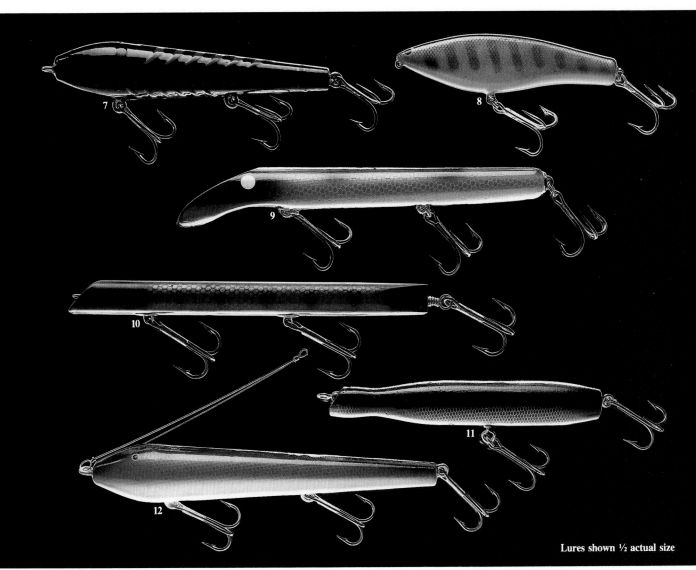

Lures shown ½ actual size

clude the following: (7) Windel's Whaletail™; (8) "B"-Flat Shiner; (9) The Stalker™, which has a scooped-out face for extra wobble; (10) Wade's Wobbler; (11) Tek-Neek; (12) Big Jerk (Teddie's Bait).

# Fishing With Jerkbaits

Many experts rate jerkbaits as the number-one lure for muskies and big pike. Although seldom used for other fish, jerkbaits sometimes take trophy-class walleyes and largemouth bass by accident.

A jerkbait appeals to big gamefish mainly because of its erratic action. As predator fish grow larger, they become lazier, and a baitfish moving erratically signals an easy meal.

You can rip a jerkbait through sparse weeds, retrieve it over weed tops or work it near a dropoff. After casting, reel up enough line so that the plug points straight toward you. Continue reeling while making sharp sweeps that can vary from 6 to 36 inches in length.

## How to Doctor a Jerkbait

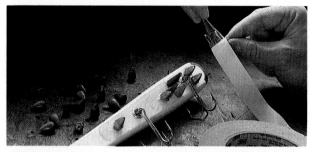

DETERMINE the proper weight distribution by attaching sinkers to the belly with double-faced tape.

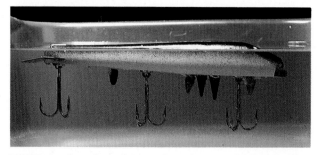

TEST the flotation of your plug after attaching the sinkers by placing it in a tub of water. Continue taping sinkers in different positions until the plug floats level with its back barely out of the water.

DRILL holes exactly where the sinkers were attached. If using cone sinkers, drill a small hole for the nose, then drill out the top of the hole for the base. Partially fill the holes with epoxy, seat the sinkers, then seal.

A high-buoyancy jerkbait rises quickly, so you must retrieve with closely-spaced jerks to keep it from floating to the surface. Most fishermen find they can jerk more quickly with the rod tip pointing downward rather than sideways. When fished this way, these plugs dive rapidly, moving up and down more than side to side.

A low-buoyancy jerkbait will not dive as steeply. Short, sharp jerks will give it a side-to-side action; long, smooth jerks will give it an up and down, gliding action. Because the plug glides farther with each jerk and does not rise as quickly, the jerks can be more widely spaced. Ideally, the plug should follow a zigzag path 2 to 3 feet wide.

Experiment with the length and timing of your jerks to find the pattern that works best. Often a series of 2- to 3-inch tugs between longer jerks will trigger the fish to strike.

Casting is by far the most popular method for presenting jerkbaits, but trolling can also be effective. Motor along the edge of a weedbed while sweeping your rod sideways. Adjust your trolling speed to suit the action of the plug.

Some fishermen doctor their jerkbaits, especially high-buoyancy models, to make them run deeper, glide farther, and float back to the surface more slowly. A doctored plug will often draw strikes from fish that ignore standard models. And you do not have to jerk as frantically to keep the plug from rising to the surface.

Setting the hook with a jerkbait is more difficult than with other plugs. Slack forms after each jerk, and unless you reel up the loose line immediately, you will not be able to get enough leverage. Even if your line is tight, you may have difficulty. When a big pike or muskie clamps onto your jerkbait, only an extremely strong pull will break the fish's grip and move the plug far enough to sink the hooks.

To set the hook this hard, you need a very stiff rod. Jerkbaits may weigh as much as 4 ounces, so a stiff rod is also necessary for casting and retrieving them properly. A rod with a long handle provides extra leverage for casting and setting the hook.

Most fishermen use 30- to 50-pound dacron line on a sturdy, free-spool reel. Dacron line will not stretch and cause you to lose hook-setting power. If your jerkbait comes with a leader attached, additional snaps or leaders are unnecessary. If it does not have a leader, attach a solid-wire or multi-strand wire leader of at least 45-pound test.

A common mistake in fishing with jerkbaits is horsing the fish after you set the hook. With a stiff rod and heavy, non-stretch line, you can easily rip the hook loose unless you play the fish carefully.

*Tips for Fishing With Jerkbaits*

BEND the metal tail down slightly to make the plug dive more sharply. Bend one side of the tail down to make the plug veer more to that side.

PLACE a strip of fluorescent tape on the back of your jerkbait. The tape helps you see the plug in the water so you can control its action.

STORE jerkbaits and other large lures by pushing the hooks into the lip of a styrofoam cooler. The lures dry quickly and do not snag your net.

# Soft Plastics

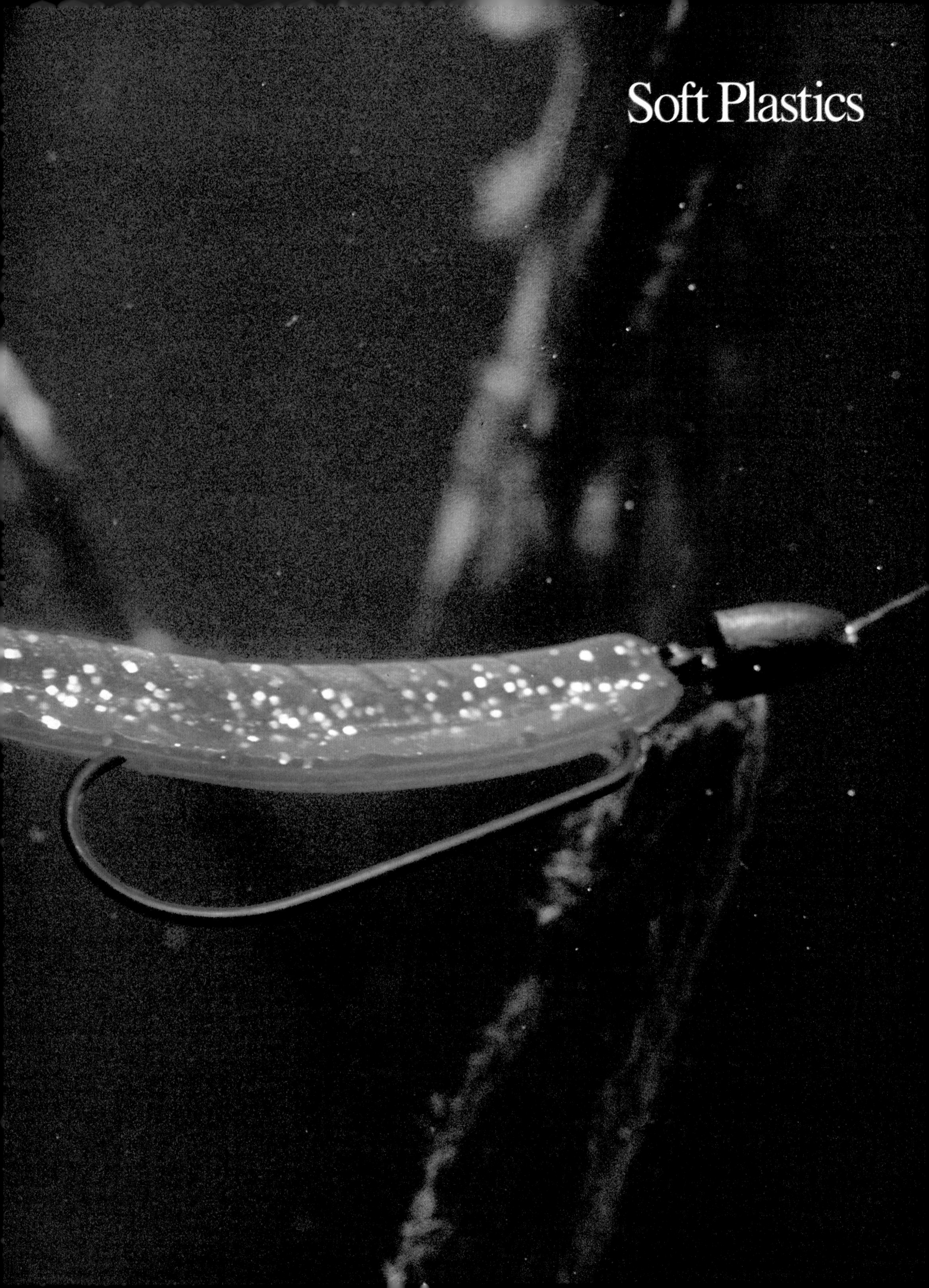

# Soft Plastics

Fishermen have used soft-bodied lures since 1860, when the first rubber worm was patented. But most of the early lures lacked the lifelike action of modern soft plastics because the material was relatively hard by today's standards.

In 1949, an Ohio luremaker began molding plastic worms from a new synthetic material, polyvinyl chloride resin. Bass fishermen who tested these lures soon reported fantastic results. Because the worms were so soft, they flexed with each twitch of the line, resulting in an irresistible action.

The popularity of soft plastics has skyrocketed since those early years. Most tackle stores now offer a wide selection of soft plastic worms, grubs, crayfish, shrimp, frogs, snakes, lizards, salamanders, salmon eggs, and adult and larval insect imitations. Today, fishermen use soft plastic lures for virtually all species of gamefish.

Soft plastics offer several major advantages over hard-bodied lures. A hard-bodied artificial does not have a texture like real food, so fish may immediately recognize it as a fake and eject it. If you do not set the hook instantly, you will probably miss the fish. But a soft plastic has a lifelike texture, so fish will mouth it an instant longer, giving you extra time to set the hook.

Many soft plastics can be rigged with the hook point buried inside where it cannot catch on obstructions. This way, a soft plastic can be retrieved through dense weeds or brush, or over rocks and logs with practically no chance of snagging. Yet the point will penetrate the soft material when you set the hook.

Another attribute of soft plastics is the ability to absorb scents. You can treat soft plastics with bottled fish attractants or buy them with scents molded in. Scents quickly wash off hard-bodied lures, but soft plastic holds scent much longer.

Often, soft plastics look almost exactly like natural fish foods. Legs, feelers, and even minute details like scales add to the realistic appearance. Many have translucent bodies which allow light to pass through, much as it passes through common foods like baitfish, worms, shrimp, and insect larvae.

Modern soft plastics vary in hardness from almost jellylike to relatively firm. The softer lures look and feel more natural to fish. But the harder ones are more durable, and stay on the hook better, especially when fished in snaggy cover. Most manufacturers use a plastic between these extremes.

To cast the smallest soft plastic lures, you will need light spinning tackle with sinkers or a plastic bubble. Or, you can use fly tackle. To cast plastic worms less than 6 inches long, light spinning tackle and 4- to 8-pound mono usually work best. For larger worms with exposed hooks, most fishermen prefer spinning or bait-casting tackle with lines from 8- to 15-pound test. For larger worms with hooks buried in the plastic, use bait-casting tackle with lines from 12- to 25-pound test.

Some manufacturers make powerful rods, called *worm rods*, specifically for driving the hook point through a soft plastic lure and into a fish's jaw. When working soft plastics through weeds or brush, use abrasion-resistant line.

# Plastic Worms

The amazing success of the plastic worm results not only from its tantalizing action, but from its ability to snake through the densest cover without snagging. Rigged Texas-style (page 83), a worm works better than any other lure for probing thick weeds, brush

or flooded timber. And if the worm does become snagged, you can break it off and tie on a new one for only a few pennies.

Color is an important consideration in choosing plastic worms. Opinions differ greatly, but most largemouth bass fishermen prefer purple, blue or black worms. Other popular choices include red, green and motor oil. Motor-oil worms change color as the light strikes them at different angles, much the same way a film of oil on water changes color. Metal-flake and fire-tail worms often draw more strikes than worms in solid colors.

Shape is also important. Most worms come with long, cylindrical bodies, but the shape of the tail varies greatly. Curly-tails wiggle enticingly when retrieved and are an excellent choice in current. Auger-tails have a long flattened tail with a single twist, causing a wild, gyrating action. Curly-tails and

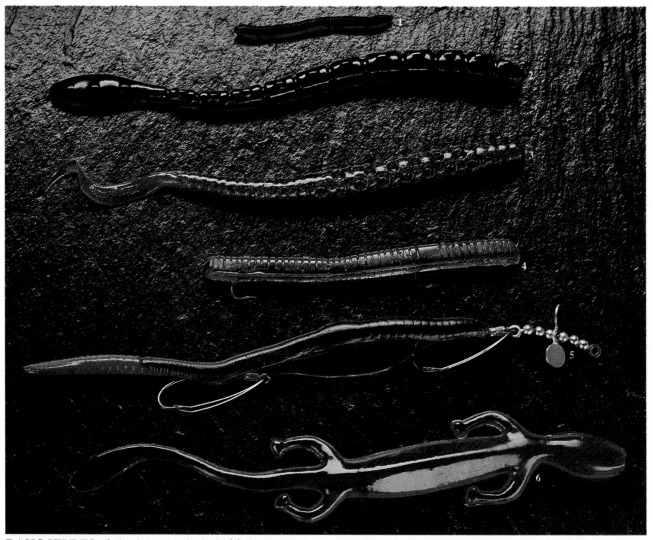

BASIC STYLES of plastic worms include (1) short, thin-bodied worms used mainly for panfish; (2) standard worms for larger gamefish; (3) worms that release air bubbles in the water; (4) pre-rigged worms; (5) pre-rigged worms with spinner blades; and (6) lizard-like worms with arms and legs.

auger-tails sink more slowly than other worms. Paddle-tails have a good swimming action when fished with a jigging retrieve. Straight-tails have less action than other types. They work best for tying threaded multiple-hook rigs (page 83).

Size of the worm depends not only on the species of fish, but on the time of year and the water clarity. Small worms usually work best in spring, before the water warms. Larger worms are a better choice in summer, when fish become more active. Small worms are generally best in clear water; larger worms in murky water.

Buoyancy can also be a consideration. A worm that rides above bottom is easily visible to fish and less prone to snagging. And, you need the buoyancy when floating a worm on the surface. Most plastic worms will float, but many are not buoyant enough to float when rigged with a worm hook. When

flotation is important, use a worm made from highly buoyant material or one with air pockets molded in.

Most plastic worms come without hooks, so you can rig them to suit your fishing situation. A few worms come pre-rigged with a monofilament hook harness threaded into the body. This type of rigging works well when fish are striking short. But pre-rigged worms snag easily and generally lack the action of other worms.

When rigging Texas-style, choose a hook with a long, sharp point that will easily penetrate the worm. The shaft must be bent at the proper angle for good penetration, and should have barbs or sharp bends to keep the worm from sliding back when you set the hook. With a Carolina rig (page 83), use a plain, straight-shank hook; a hook with a light wire weedguard; or the same type of hook used for Texas-style rigging.

TAIL SHAPE determines the action of a plastic worm. Popular tail designs include (1) curly tail or twister tail, (2) auger tail, (3) paddle tail or flap tail, (4) straight tail, and (5) skirted tail, on tube-style worm.

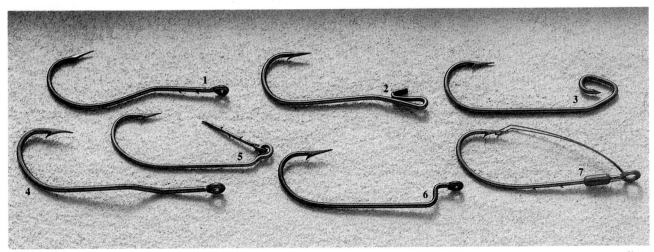

POPULAR HOOKS for Texas-style rigging include: (1) VMC Faultless, (2) Lindy Sure-Lok, (3) Worth Worm-Loc, (4) Tru-Turn 772, (5) Mister Twister Keeper, and (6) Eagle Claw 95 JB. You can also rig a worm on a weedless hook like the (7) Eagle Claw 449 WA. Special hooks are unnecessary when rigging with the hook point exposed.

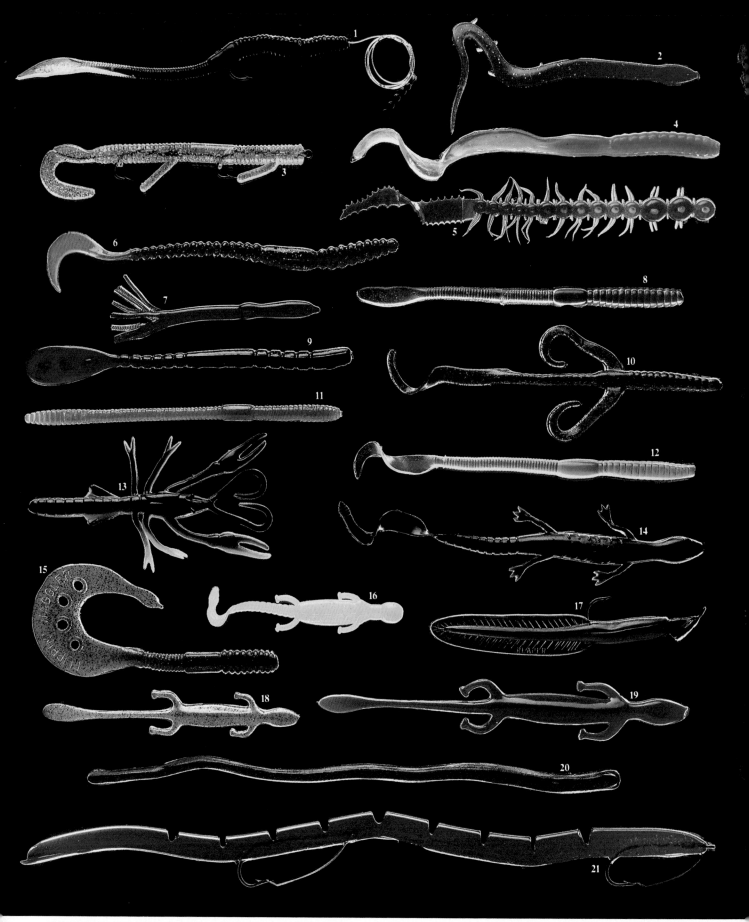

PLASTIC WORMS include: (1) Swimmin' Worm, (2) Salt Snakey, (3) Limit Finder, (4) Culprit®, (5) Hawg Hackle, (6) Jiggle Tail, (7) The Tube®, (8) Super Scamp™, (9) Vibrator, (10) Salty Sensation, (11) Chumm'n™ Worm, (12) Alamance Curl Tail, (13) Poc'it Dad, (14) Spoiler® Lizard, (15) Flippin' Waggler, (16) Fliptail® Baby Creature, (17) Method Reaper®, (18) Woodie Worm, (19) Producto Lizard, (20) S.S.T. Whopper, (21)

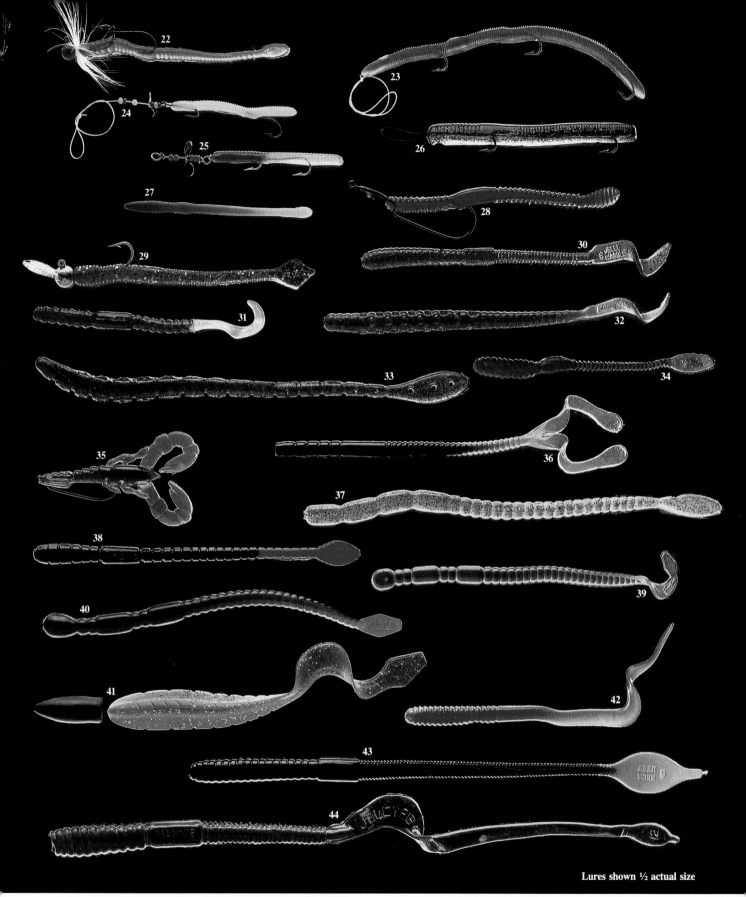

Hawg Hunter®, (22) Water Crawler, (23) Bass Stopper, (24) Angle Worm, (25) Blakemore Worm Rig, (26) Do-Nothing®, (27) Midjit Crawler, (28) Slider, (29) Mean Machine®, (30) Jelly Waggler®, (31) Curly Macho, (32) Poc'it Phenom, (33) Shur-Hooker, (34) Wiggle Bit, (35) Cajun Crawdad®, (36) Renegade, (37) Squealer®, (38) Shimmy Babe®, (39) Feisty, (40) Fliptail®, (41) Fandango, (42) Super Snake, (43) Jelly Worm®, (44) Augertail®.

# Fishing With Plastic Worms

A hungry largemouth finds it difficult to resist a plastic worm squirming seductively through its underwater hideout. Plastic worms appeal most strongly to largemouth bass, but also work for smallmouth and spotted bass, sunfish, northern pike, walleyes and even brown trout.

Worms used for sunfish usually measure 2 to 3 inches long; for smallmouth and spotted bass, walleyes and brown trout, 4 to 6 inches; for most largemouth bass, 6 to 8 inches; and for northern pike and big largemouths, 9 to 13 inches.

For bass and sunfish, plastic worms work best starting when the water temperature reaches 60°F in spring and continuing until the temperature drops below 60°F in fall. Worms remain effective at cooler temperatures for most other species.

Fishing with plastic worms bears many similarities to fishing with jigs. Fish usually grab a plastic worm as it sinks, so you need a sensitive touch to detect a strike. You must keep your line taut as the worm drops, or strikes will go unnoticed.

The way you rig your plastic worm depends on the fishing situation. For fishing in weeds, brush, timber, or other dense cover, rig your worm Texas-style. Because the hook point is buried inside the plastic, you can retrieve the worm over obstructions without snagging.

You can also rig your worm on a weedless single hook when fishing in heavy cover. Because the point is exposed, you can set the hook more easily. But worms rigged this way catch more debris than those rigged Texas-style.

When snags are not a problem, thread your worm on a jig head with a barbed collar, or use a multiple-hook rig. The exposed hooks will improve your hooking percentage.

The Carolina rig is a good choice for deep-water trolling. The swivel prevents the line from twisting as it would if you trolled with a Texas rig.

When rigging Texas- or Carolina-style, use a hook from size #2 to 1/0 with a 4-inch worm; 1/0 to 3/0 with a 6-inch worm; 4/0 or 5/0 with an 8-inch worm; and 5/0 or 6/0 with a 10- to 13-inch worm.

A common mistake in rigging plastic worms Texas-style is to use too much weight. A worm slithering slowly draws more strikes than one sinking rapidly. With a standard 6-inch worm, a ⅛-ounce sinker is usually adequate at depths of 10 feet or less. Seldom will you need a sinker weighing more than ¼ ounce. When trolling with a Carolina rig in deep water, use a sinker of ½ ounce or more.

Inexperienced worm fishermen often use rods that are too soft, so they fail to set the hook hard enough. To drive the hook point through the plastic and into a fish's jaw, use a stiff graphite or boron worm rod. When you detect a strike, lower the rod tip and reel up the slack rapidly, then set the hook as hard as you can. Expert fishermen often set the hook two or three times to make sure it sinks in.

## How to Rig a Plastic Worm Texas-style

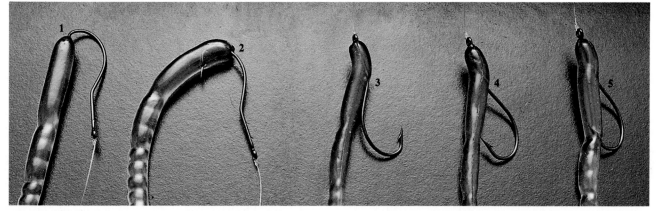

TEXAS-RIG a plastic worm by (1) inserting the point of the hook into the head end. (2) Push the hook about ½ inch into the head, then out the side. (3) Continue pushing the hook through the worm, leaving only the eye protruding. (4) Twist the hook one-half turn. (5) Push the hook into the worm until the point almost penetrates the opposite side. The rigged worm should hang straight with no kinks or twists.

## How to Tie a Multiple-hook Rig

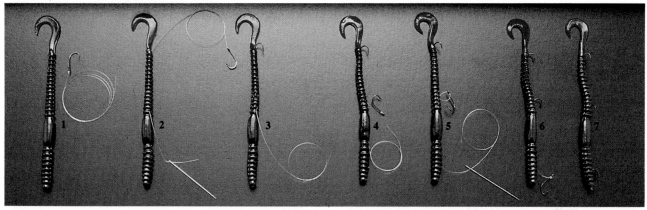

TIE (1) a length of 6-pound mono to a #6 hook. (2) With a needle, thread the line into the tail and out the middle of a 6-inch worm. (3) Pull the line to draw the hook into the worm. (4) Tie on another hook using a nail knot (page 13). (5) Thread the line into the same hole, then out a hook's length behind the head. (6) Pull the middle hook into the worm, then nail-knot a third hook to the mono; trim. (7) Push the hook, eye first, into the hole, then up to the tip of the head. The mono inside the worm should be taut, but not tight enough to kink the worm.

## Other Rigging Methods

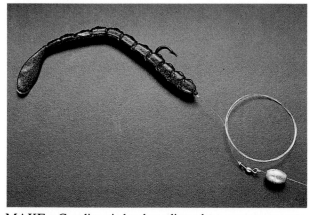

MAKE a Carolina rig by threading a buoyant worm onto a barbed-shank hook, leaving the point exposed. Or, use a worm hook and bury the point. Tie the hook to an 18- to 36-inch leader attached to a slip-sinker rig.

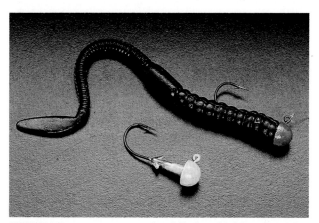

THREAD a worm onto a lead jig head with a strongly-barbed collar. Push firmly to snug the worm against the jig head so there is no gap. Mushroom-head jigs work especially well for this type of rigging.

HOP a Texas-rigged worm through timber, brush or dense weeds. If the worm catches on an obstruction, twitch the rod to free it. To prevent the sinker from sliding away from the worm, peg the sinker in place by wedging a piece of toothpick into the hole.

SKIP a plastic worm under a dock or other overhanging cover to reach bass hiding in the shade. Keep your rod tip low, then snap your wrist sharply. To avoid a backlash when the worm hits the water, use spinning instead of bait-casting tackle.

FLIP a Texas-rigged worm so it lands alongside a tree trunk or in any hard-to-reach spot. Keep your line taut as the worm sinks and be ready to set the hook at any sign of a twitch or pause. When using this technique, most fishermen prefer a stiff rod about 7½ feet long.

RETRIEVE a 2- to 3-inch plastic worm along the edge of submerged weeds or over weedtops to catch sunfish. Use a #6 or #8 hook and leave the point exposed. If the fish are striking short, use a multiple-hook rig (page 83) with two #8 hooks.

RIG a plastic worm on a jig head when fishing over weedtops or along a weedline. If the open hook catches on vegetation, jerk sharply to free it. Use a jig head with a double-barbed collar to prevent the worm from slipping back when you jerk.

CRAWL an unweighted plastic worm over pads or other surface vegetation. Retrieve with twitches and pauses. Use a highly buoyant worm and a small hook for maximum flotation. You may need lighter-than-normal line to cast the nearly weightless rig.

*Tips for Fishing With Plastic Worms*

CUT a small slit in the back half of a plastic worm, then insert a small piece of a seltzer tablet. Bubbles from the fizzing tablet attract gamefish, which then strike the worm.

SLOW the sink rate of a plastic worm by (1) filing a groove in a cone sinker. (2) Tie on live rubber, then (3) stretch it while cutting to length. The rubber forms a (4) skirt around the sinker.

AVOID storing worms or other soft plastics with painted lures, plastic hook or swivel boxes, or worms of different colors. The resin eats the paint or plastic, and the colors bleed.

# Lifelike Soft Plastics

The amazingly lifelike look of many soft plastics can be easily explained: they are made from molds of the real thing.

Live-bait fishermen would argue that even the best imitation can never be as effective as the genuine food item. But most would agree that soft plastics offer some advantages over live bait.

The major advantage is durability. Live bait often tears away from the hook when you cast, and a short-striking fish can easily steal your bait. Imitations stay on the hook much better, although toothy fish may occasionally nip off the tail.

Many of the best live baits are not available at bait shops. Rather than collecting their own bait and making provisions to keep it alive, many fishermen opt for soft plastics.

Soft plastic insect imitations work best for panfish and trout; plastic eggs for salmon and steelhead; crayfish for bass and trout; and frogs and waterdogs for bass, northern pike and walleyes. Baitfish imitations catch most types of freshwater gamefish.

Many lifelike soft plastics come unrigged. Fishermen thread them on hooks or fish them on lead jig heads (page 98). Some, including almost all insect imitations, come with a hook molded into the plastic or rigged with a hook harness.

*How to Rig Lifelike Soft Plastics*

RIG a plastic egg by (1) pushing it onto the point of an egg hook; or (2) onto the hook of a yarn fly, over the fly, then onto the line. Rig an egg cluster on a (3) sliced-shank hook or (4) treble hook with one point exposed. Rig a plastic frog or waterdog by (5) pushing the point of a worm hook into the nose, out one-half inch behind the nose, then through the back; or (6) threading it onto a hook with a light-wire weedguard.

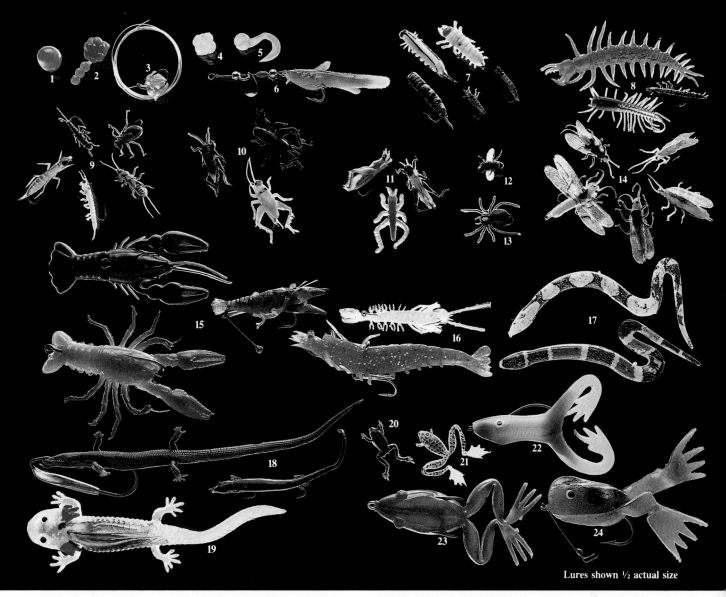

LIFELIKE SOFT PLASTICS include (1) Jensenegg, (2) Super Spawn, (3) Gooey Bob®, (4) Trout Treats, (5) Li'l Fry, (6) Stonecat, (7) grubs, (8) hellgrammites, (9) other nymphs, (10) crickets, (11) grasshoppers, (12) Bee, (13) Spider, (14) adult aquatic insects, (15) crayfish, (16) shrimp, (17) snakes, (18) lizards, (19) Waterdog, (20) Creme Frog, (21) T's Ribbet, (22) Hawg Frawg, (23) Snagproof Frog, (24) Super Frog.

*Techniques for Fishing With Lifelike Soft Plastics*

SLOW-TROLL or drift with a 1½- to 2-inch soft plastic crayfish on a slip-sinker rig for smallmouth and spotted bass. The buoyant crayfish will ride above bottom so the hook cannot snag in rocks or bottom debris.

CAST a floating or sinking insect imitation on a plastic bubble rig to catch sunfish and other panfish. Twitch the bubble over the weedtops, pausing several seconds between twitches.

# Jigs & Jigging Lures

# Jigs & Jigging Lures

Many expert fishermen consider jigs and jigging lures the most consistently productive of all artificial lures. They work for a wide variety of species under almost any conditions.

A jig is simply a piece of lead with a hook molded into it. A dressing of hair, feathers, tinsel or soft plastic generally conceals the hook. Other types of jigging lures include the jigging spoon, a very thick metal spoon; the vibrating blade, a thin metal minnow imitation; and the tailspin, a lead-bodied lure with a spinner at the rear.

Jigs and jigging lures can be fished slowly, so they work especially well in cold water. Low water temperature reduces the metabolic rate of fish, making them reluctant to chase fast-moving lures. But the slow jigging action will often tempt a strike.

The rapid sink rate of most jigs and jigging lures makes them an excellent choice for reaching bottom in current or for fishing in deep water. Lake trout anglers, for example, regularly use these lures at depths up to 100 feet with no extra weight added to the line. But jigs and jigging lures can also be effective in water only a few feet deep.

Most jigs and jigging lures have compact bodies, so they are ideal for casting into the wind or for casting long distances. The extra distance helps you take fish in clear water or in other situations where they are easily spooked.

Despite the effectiveness of jigs and jigging lures, many anglers have difficulty catching fish with them. The main problem is detecting the strike. Fish seldom slam these lures as they do a crankbait or surface lure. Instead, they inhale the lure gently, usually as it settles toward bottom. If you are not alert or do not have a taut line as the lure sinks, you will not notice the strike.

Because strikes are often light, jigs and jigging lures should be fished with sensitive tackle. Most experts prefer a relatively stiff graphite or boron rod, with just enough flexibility in the tip to cast the lure.

Ultra-light to medium-power spinning or light baitcasting outfits work well in most cases. But heavier tackle is needed to handle lures over ¾ ounce or to horse fish from heavy cover.

Use the lightest line practical for the species and fishing conditions. If your line is too heavy, the lure will sink too slowly and will not stay at the desired depth when retrieved. Also, strikes will be more difficult to detect.

With ordinary monofilament, the twitch signalling a strike is hard to see. To detect strikes more easily, use fluorescent monofilament. Many jig fishermen wear polarized sunglasses to improve line visibility even more.

When selecting jigs and jigging lures, the main consideration is weight. Your selection must be a compromise based on the type of fish, water depth, current speed and wind velocity.

For panfish, most anglers prefer lures of no more than ⅛ ounce. Some panfish jigs, called *micro jigs,* weigh as little as ¹⁄₈₀ ounce. For mid-sized gamefish like walleyes and bass, ¼- to ½-ounce lures normally work best. For larger gamefish, lures of 1 ounce or more are usually most productive.

The lure must be heavy enough to reach the desired depth, but not so heavy that it sinks too fast. Fish usually prefer a slowly falling lure to one plummeting toward bottom. As a general rule, allow ⅛ ounce for every 10 feet of water. For example, a lure of at least ¼ ounce would be needed to reach bottom in water 20 feet deep.

In slow current, however, the same ¼-ounce lure would only reach a depth of about 15 feet. As the current becomes faster, the weight of lure needed to reach bottom increases. Wind affects your lure choice much the same way as current. The wind pushes your boat across the surface, increasing water resistance on the line and lure. This makes it more difficult for the lure to reach the desired depth and stay there.

POPULAR HEAD DESIGNS include (1) ball; (2) keel; (3) bullet; (4) slider; (5) mushroom; (6) banana; (7) stand-up; (8) pyramid; (9) lip style, or *wiggler;* (10) spinner style or *pony;* and (11) propeller style.

# Jigs

The way a jig performs depends not only on its weight, but on its head design, the type of dressing and the hook style.

HEAD DESIGN. The head shape and position of the hook eye affect a jig's sink rate, action, and resistance to snagging or tangling in weeds. Following are the most popular head designs:

*Ball* — This common, fast-sinking head works well in most situations. But the hook eye, which is on top, tends to catch weeds.

*Keel* — Flattened vertically, this thin head slices through the water with little resistance and sinks rapidly. It is ideal for fast current or deep water.

*Bullet* — Another fast-sinking design, the bullet head cuts easily through current. Because it does not settle as rapidly as a keel head when jigged, it snags less and is usually more appealing to fish.

*Slider* — A slider head is flattened horizontally, so it sinks slowly and glides through the water. It is most effective in shallow water and for suspended fish.

*Mushroom* — This head was designed for use with soft plastic tails. The plastic can be snugged up flush to the head, and a double barb on the collar keeps it from sliding back. This makes it a good choice for ripping through weeds.

*Banana* — Because the hook eye is far forward on this head, the tail points up when you lower the lure and down when you raise it. The sharp kicking action makes this head ideal for vertical jigging.

*Stand-up* — This head is designed so that the tail and hook stand up when the jig rests on bottom. The high-riding hook makes the jig fairly snag-resistant.

*Pyramid* — The hook eye is at the front tip of the tapered head, so weeds tend to slide over the head instead of catching on the eye.

*Other head styles* — Some heads have a lip which gives the jig a wiggling action. Others have a spinner blade or propeller for extra flash and sound.

DRESSING. The type of dressing affects the sink rate and action of a jig. Most jigs come with some type of natural or synthetic dressing. Plain jig heads are used only in combination with live bait. Following are the most popular jig dressings:

*Hair* — Natural hair gives a jig an attractive pulsing action. And hair is durable, enabling you to catch many fish on the same jig. Bucktail hair works especially well. It holds its shape and its natural buoyancy slows the sink rate, making the action more tantalizing. Other popular types of hair include calf tail, squirrel tail and rabbit.

*Feathers* — Airy feathers such as marabou have an enticing, breathing action unlike that of any other material. Stiffer feathers are used as tails or hackle collars. But feathers lack the durability of hair.

*Soft plastic* — These dressings feel like real food, so a fish may mouth the jig longer before recognizing it as a fake. This extra instant improves your chances of setting the hook. And like bucktail, soft plastic slows a jig's sink rate.

Curly-tailed soft plastics wiggle enticingly. Other soft plastics imitate natural foods like minnows, crayfish and grubs.

Soft plastic tails are less durable than most other dressings. They tear after catching a few fish, and a pike, muskie or walleye can easily bite them off.

*Other dressings* — Tinsel and mylar tails are extremely durable and reflect light well. Live-rubber tails have a billowing action, and their buoyancy causes the jig to sink slowly. Imitation-hair tails made of nylon or other synthetics are tough, but mat easily and lack the action of real hair.

Fishermen sometimes combine the regular jig dressings with pork rind trailers, minnows or a wide variety of other live baits.

HOOK STYLE. How well a hook penetrates and holds a fish and how easily it unsnags depends mainly on its thickness. Most jigs come with fine-wire Aberdeen hooks that penetrate easily. When snagged, they can often be straightened with a direct pull on the line. Heavier O'Shaughnessy-style hooks work better for tough-jawed fish and for horsing fish out of dense cover.

Some hooks have a *brushguard* made of nylon bristles, a *Y*-shaped plastic strip or a piece of heavy mono.

Dina-Mite Jelly Belly

Cutie Pie

Pop-Eyed Tumble Bug

Hackle-Tail

Flu-Flu

Pink Head Tinsel

Windel's Rabbit Hair

Panfish Killer

Road Runner

Crappie Queen

Micro Jig

Gumpy

Flasher

Puddle Jumper

Binkelman's Ball

Crappie Slider

No-Alibi

Tiny Tube

Wiggle Jig

Shineee Hineee

Pinky Jig

Glo Jig

Quiver Jig

Krappie Kat

Super Shad

Fuzz-E-Grub

Fish Hawk

Whistler

Chippewa Jig Fly

Hybrid Bait Jig

Dingo Jig

Whirly Bee

Walleye Jig

Nature Jig

Twister Meeny

Hair Raiser

Vibrotail

Sassy Shad

Wigly Flipper

Bill's Keel

Gopher Bait Jig

Sting Ray Grub

Sassy Shiner

Method Reaper

Flippin' Fool

Doll Fly

Bill's Bullet

Uncle Buck's Buck 'n' Rubber

Shad Dart

Bill's Lake Trout

Stanley Jig

HammerTail

Beetle

Tinsel Tail

Arkie Bucktail

Lil' John

Flare Hair

Super Jig

Tweetle Bug

Forage Minnow

Bonefish Demon

Bill's Split-Tail

Lures shown ½ actual size

Dina-Mite Jelly Belly

Cutie Pie

Pop-Eyed Tumble Bug

Hackle-Tail

Flu-Flu

Pink Head Tinsel

Windel's Rabbit Hair

Panfish Killer

Road Runner

Crappie Queen

Micro Jig

Gumpy

Flasher

Puddle Jumper

Binkelman's Ball

Crappie Slider

No-Alibi

Tiny Tube

Wiggle Jig

Shineee Hineee

Pinky Jig

Glo Jig

Quiver Jig

Krappie Kat

Super Shad

Fuzz-E-Grub

Fish Hawk

Whistler

Chippewa Jig Fly

Hybrid Bait Jig

Dingo Jig

Whirly Bee

Walleye Jig

Nature Jig

Twister Meeny

Hair Raiser

Vibrotail

Sassy Shad

Wigly Flipper

Bill's Keel

Gopher Bait Jig

Sting Ray Grub

Sassy Shiner

Method Reaper

Flippin' Fool

Doll Fly

Bill's Bullet

Uncle Buck's Buck 'n' Rubber

Shad Dart

Bill's Lake Trout

Stanley Jig

HammerTail

Beetle

Tinsel Tail

Arkie Bucktail

Lil' John

Flare Hair

Super Jig

Tweetle Bug

Forage Minnow

Bonefish Demon

Bill's Split-Tail

Lures shown ½ actual size

# Fishing With Jigs

With the right jig and the right presentation, you can catch everything from quarter-pound sunfish to 40-pound lake trout.

The most common way to fish a jig is to cast to a likely spot, then retrieve in short hops along bottom. Another effective method is to jig vertically in tight spots or while drifting with the wind or current. When fish are suspended, you can count your jig down to different depths until you find the most productive level.

You can also troll with jigs. Slow trolling along structure will take a wide variety of fish including walleyes, northern pike, and largemouth and smallmouth bass. As you move along, twitch your rod tip to hop the jig over the bottom. Trolling steadily in mid-water will catch fish like white bass, stripers and crappies. When using this method, add a soft plastic curly-tail to your jig to improve its action.

Many anglers believe jigs are effective only on a clean bottom because they snag easily in brush and foul in weeds. But a light jig works well when hopped over weed or brush tops. With a little practice, you can keep it dancing inches above the cover.

Tipping your jig with live bait like minnows, worms, leeches, or insect larvae will often improve your results. But you may have to use a stinger hook (page 99) to catch short strikers.

Catching fish on jigs requires a high level of concentration, a fine-tuned sense of feel and quick reflexes. If you fail to pay constant attention, if you are not accustomed to recognizing subtle strikes, or if you do not set the hook immediately, chances are you will go home with an empty stringer.

You can improve your jig-fishing skills by following these guidelines:

- Keep your line taut at all times, especially as the jig sinks. But the line should not be so tight that it interferes with the action of the jig.

- Stay alert for any twitch or sideways movement of the line.

- Watch your line carefully to make sure the jig sinks normally after the cast and when jigging. If it stops sinking unexpectedly, a fish has probably grabbed it.

- Set the hook at the slightest indication of a strike. Do not hesitate; a fish can pick up the jig and expel it in an instant.

Always tie your jig directly to the line, without snaps, swivels or other connectors. A loop knot like the Duncan loop (page 12) will allow the jig to swing freely, maximizing its action. When fishing for northern pike, pickerel or muskies, attach a wire striker to your jig using a twist-melt connection or haywire twist (page 14).

Most serious jig fishermen carry a jig box stocked with a wide variety of heads and dressings for different species and situations. Often, a head weighing 1/8 ounce more or less than the one you are using can make a big difference.

*Basic Bottom-bouncing Technique*

CAST your jig past the fish zone, then (1) pay out line as the jig sinks. When the jig hits bottom,(2) your line will go slack. Tighten your line slightly, then (3) twitch the rod tip to make the jig hop forward. As the jig sinks, (4) lower the rod tip slowly to keep the line taut. Keeping a taut line at this point is the key to success with this technique. Continue to hop the jig this way until you can no longer maintain contact with bottom.

REEL a spinner-type jig steadily over logs or brush in shallow water. The resistance of the blade reduces the sink rate, so you can retrieve slowly without snagging. This technique is best for bass and crappies.

TIP a plain, fluorescent-colored jighead with a minnow, leech or piece of nightcrawler when fish refuse to strike dressed jigs. The fluorescent head draws attention from fish, and the plain hook will not hide the bait.

HOP a stand-up jig over a snaggy bottom. The hook seldom hangs up because the jig usually comes to rest with the tail pointing upward. And the upright tail is easy for fish to see.

RIP a pyramid or mushroom jig through sparse weeds or along the edges of thicker patches. When the jig hits weeds, jerk your rod sharply with a snap of the wrists to tear it loose. A short, stout rod works best.

SUSPEND a micro jig from a pencil float to fish over brush or weeds. Twitch the float so the jig rises, then settles back to the cover. Set the hook when the float tips up. This method works especially well for crappies.

FLIP a brushguard jig alongside a tree or into a tight pocket in weeds or brush. Flippin' enables you to fish targets quickly and accurately. A banana-head jig dressed with a pork strip is ideal for this technique.

*Jig Sink Rate (sink rate measured in feet per second)*

| HEAD STYLE | | JIG WEIGHT | | | | | |
|---|---|---|---|---|---|---|---|
| | | ⅛ ounce | ¼ ounce | ⅜ ounce | ½ ounce | ¾ ounce | 1 ounce |
| | Ball | 2.4 | 3.5 | 4.4 | 5.2 | 6.1 | 6.4 |
| | Keel | — | 3.2 | 4.1 | 4.6 | 5.5 | 6.0 |
| | Bullet | 2.2 | 3.3 | 4.0 | 4.6 | 5.5 | 5.9 |
| | Slider | 1.7 | 2.0 | 1.5* | — | — | — |
| | Mushroom | 2.2 | 3.3 | 3.9 | 4.4 | — | — |
| | Banana | — | 2.9 | 3.3 | 3.7 | 4.4 | 4.9 |
| | Stand-up | — | 3.3 | 3.9 | 4.4 | — | — |
| | Pyramid | 2.3 | 3.4 | 4.0 | 4.6 | — | — |

NOTES: All sink rates were measured with jig heads tied to 6-pound test line • Only commonly available weights were tested • All jig heads were tested without dressing. Dressed jigs normally sink 5 to 10% slower.
*Sink rate slower than expected due to flattened jig head trapping an air bubble.

## How to Rig Soft Plastic Dressings

SELECT a (1) jig head with large barbs on the collar. The barbs keep the tail from sliding back each time you attempt to set the hook. To rig a (2) curly tail, center the hook on the front of the body and push it through so that only the bend and point protrude. Insert the hook into a (3) shad and out through the midline of the back. Be sure the hook penetrates the back, not the belly. Rig a (4) crayfish on a slider head by pushing the hook through the

## Tips for Using Jigs

ANCHOR a soft plastic tail to the jig head to keep the tail from sliding back. Apply a drop of super glue to the collar, then push the tail forward. Let the glue dry before using the jig.

MOLD your own jigs using tin rather than lead. A tin jig sinks more slowly than a lead jig of the same size and shape. And, the tin has a permanent shine that appeals to many gamefish.

SHORTEN your jig tail to improve your hooking percentage when fish are striking short. A jig with a shortened tail appears smaller and often draws more strikes.

CAST downstream when fishing in a river with a snaggy bottom. If your jig hangs up, allow your line to drift with the current. Continue feeding line until the belly is 20 to 30 feet below the spot where you are snagged. Point your

body, from the bottom up. The point should come out just behind the head. Press the tail over the hook eye until the eye comes through. Thread on a (5) Sassy Shiner™ so that the hook protrudes between the dorsal fins. The fins help keep the hook from fouling, making the lure semi-weedless. Position a (6) paddle-tail grub with the flat part of the tail turned horizontally. This way, the grub tail pumps up and down when you jig the lure.

TIE a #10 or 12 treble hook, or *stinger*, to the bend of your jig hook to catch short-striking fish. Pierce the head of a minnow with the jig hook; the tail with one prong of the stinger.

CHOOSE jigs with fine-wire hooks when fishing around flooded trees or stumps. The hook will straighten enough so you can free it from a snag, and you can easily bend it back.

BITE a piece from the tail of a soft plastic shad or shiner to improve its action. Reducing the thickness of the tail makes it more flexible, increasing the amount of side-to-side wiggle.

rod tip at the snag, then pull sharply with a long, sweeping motion. Water resistance against the belly of the line enables you to exert a downstream tug which usually frees the jig.

# Jigging Lures

Jigging lures, unlike most jigs, have some type of built-in action. All jigging lures can be fished with a jigging motion, and some also work well with a straight retrieve. Jigging lures are divided into the following categories:

JIGGING SPOONS. These lures resemble spoons used for casting or trolling, but are generally thicker and flatter. Most are made of lead, chromed brass or stainless steel. Because jigging spoons have treble hooks, they hang up more often than jigs. But they unsnag easily, so they are ideal for fishing in timber and brush.

Long, thin jigging spoons are used mainly for vertical jigging, but also work for casting. Shorter, wider spoons, called *slab spoons,* resemble small shad. Their compact shape makes them effective for distance casting to schools of gamefish pursuing shad on or near the surface.

VIBRATING BLADES. These lures have a lead head, a thin steel tail, and treble hooks at each end. A series of line-attachment holes enables you to change the balance and action. Vibrating blades can be used for vertical jigging, casting or trolling.

TAILSPINS. The thick lead body has a wire at the rear that serves as a shaft for a spinner blade. Most tailspins have one treble hook attached to the bottom, but some have another treble behind the spinner blade. The attachment eye is at the top. Tailspins are excellent for vertical jigging and casting to surface-schooling fish.

## *How the Action of Jigging Lures Differs*

JIGGING SPOONS flash and flutter erratically when allowed to sink on a slack line. They tip slightly from side to side when retrieved. But jigging spoons generally lack the typical wobbling action associated with most other types of spoons.

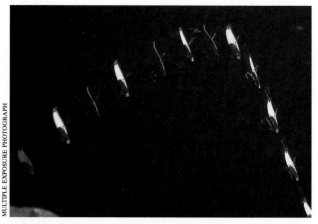

VIBRATING BLADES wiggle rapidly when pulled through the water, but have no action as they sink. Attaching the line farther to the rear increases the wiggle.

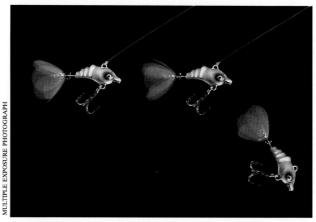

TAILSPINS have a spinner blade that turns when the lure is pulled forward and helicopters when the lure is allowed to sink. Tailspins lack the fluttering or wiggling action of other jigging lures, but the constant rotation of the blade provides more flash.

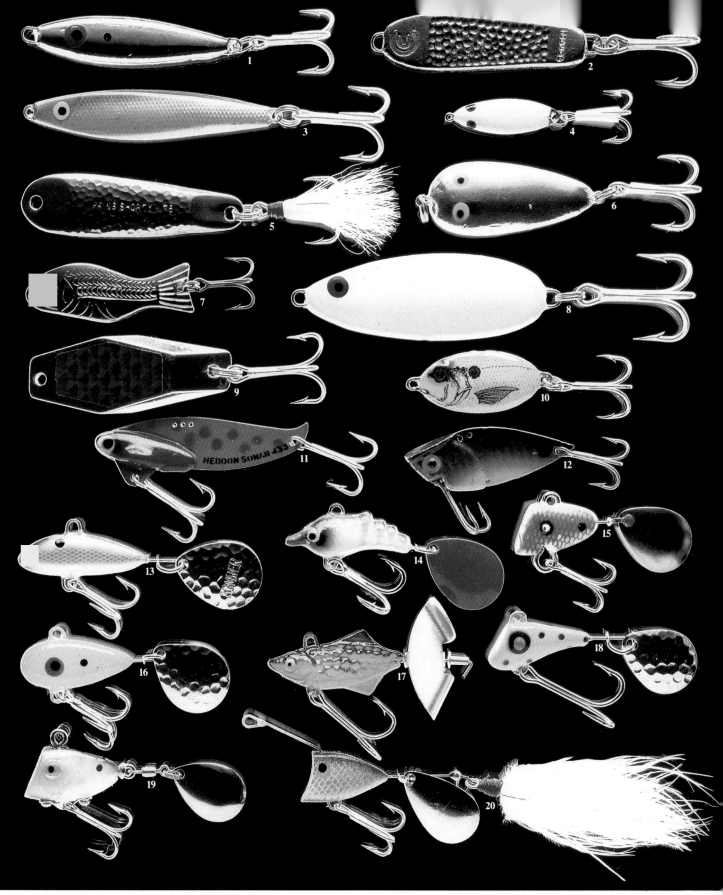

JIGGING LURES include *jigging spoons,* like: (1) Mann-O-Lure, (2) C.C. Spoon®, (3) Nördic™, (4) Stinger, (5) Hopkins Shorty®, (6) Striper Stopper, (7) Al's Goldfish, (8) Striper Slab Spoon®, (9) Diamond Champ™, (10) Slab Spoon®. Many thick spoons (page 117) will substitute for jigging spoons, and vice versa. *Vibrating blades* include: (11) Sonar™, (12) Gay Blade®. *Tailspins* include: (13) Spinner Minnow, (14) Craw George, (15) Little Suzy™, (16) Little George®, (17) Whopper Spin, (18) Pico® Pirate, (19) Spinnin Minnow, (20) Marabou Spinrite®.

## Fishing With Jigging Spoons

When fish are buried in heavy cover or holding along vertical structure, no other lure works as well as a jigging spoon. Its density causes it to sink quickly, so you can lower it into tight spots where other lures would be difficult to present.

You can jig a spoon vertically in a small opening in a stand of flooded timber, over a deep brush pile, or alongside a bridge piling or sheer cliff. Or, you can jig it vertically while drifting with the wind or current. You can also cast a jigging spoon and retrieve it along bottom, as you would a jig.

A jigging spoon has an attractive fluttering action when it sinks. But if you keep the line too tight, the spoon will not flutter. As the spoon sinks, maintain less tension than you would with a jig.

Jigging spoons are most effective when the water is cool or cold and fish hold tight to cover, refusing fast-moving lures. Under these conditions, you must work the lure slowly and present it within inches of the fish.

A fish strikes a jigging spoon much the same way it strikes a jig. Set the hook at any tap, or if the line moves sideways or fails to drop as expected.

Fishermen use spoons weighing from ⅛ to ¼ ounce for crappies and white bass; ¼ to 1 ounce for largemouth, smallmouth and spotted bass; and 1 to 2½ ounces for lake trout and stripers.

ATTACH a split ring to the eye using a split-ring pliers. Tying directly to the eye restricts the action, and the sharp edge will fray your line.

CAST a slab spoon to a surface school of white bass, stripers or largemouths. Circling gulls often pinpoint a school. Start your retrieve as soon as the spoon hits the water, and hold your rod tip high to keep the lure from sinking. A rapid retrieve usually draws more strikes than a slow one.

WORK a jigging spoon along the shady side of a standing tree or other vertical cover. Lower the spoon a few feet, then jig it at that depth for several seconds. Continue lowering and jigging until you reach bottom.

JIG the spoon vertically as you drift over a school of suspended fish. A graph recorder enables you to see the fish and the path of your spoon. Then, you can adjust your depth accordingly.

## Tips for Using Jigging Spoons

MULTIPLE EXPOSURE PHOTOGRAPH

BEND a jigging spoon to give it the best action for your type of fishing. A straight body or slight bend is adequate for vertical jigging. A more pronounced bend produces a wider wobble and works better for casting.

FREE a snagged spoon by raising your rod gently until the line is taut. Do not pull hard or the hook will sink in deeper. Drop the rod tip rapidly; the impact of the heavy spoon falling will usually dislodge the hook.

JIG a blade vertically by sweeping your rod upward to make the lure vibrate. Experiment with sweeps ranging from 1 to 4 feet, always keeping the line taut while the lure sinks. Fish almost always strike on the drop.

## Fishing With Vibrating Blades

A vibrating blade attracts gamefish with its intense wiggling action. Because fish can detect vibrating blades with their lateral-line sense as well as with their sense of sight, the lures work well even in turbid water.

Fishermen use blades weighing from ⅛ to ¼ ounce for white bass and crappies; from ¼ to ½ ounce for walleyes, largemouths and smallmouths; and from ½ to 1 ounce for stripers and lake trout.

You can fish a vibrating blade by jigging vertically, casting or trolling. Vertical jigging generally works best over a fairly clean bottom. Because a blade lacks the density of a jigging spoon, it is not as easy to free should it become snagged.

When casting or trolling with a vibrating blade, keep the lure moving steadily, much as you would with a crankbait. The fast sink rate of a blade enables you to reach deeper water than you could with most crankbaits. You can also hop a vibrating blade across bottom. The hopping retrieve is much like the bottom-bouncing technique described on page 95, but you must use longer upward sweeps to make the blade vibrate.

Vibrating blades have two or three holes along the back for attaching your line. How much the lure wiggles and the depth at which it runs depends on where you attach it. Experiment with different attachment holes to determine the one that works best for your fishing situation.

CONNECT a blade with a plain snap instead of a snap-swivel. The hooks swing up when the lure sinks and may foul on a longer swivel.

CLIP your line to the front attachment hole of a vibrating blade to produce the tightest vibration and make the lure run deepest on the retrieve (top). Connect the line to the rear hole to produce the widest wobble and make the lure run shallowest (bottom).

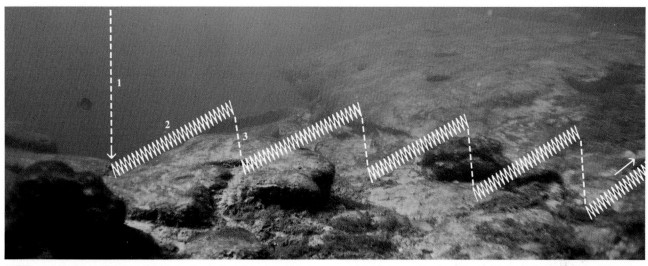

HOP a vibrating blade along bottom by first casting beyond the fish zone, then (1) paying out line as it sinks. When it hits bottom, (2) sweep your rod upward fast enough to make the blade vibrate. To detect strikes, (3) keep your line taut as the lure sinks. Continue hopping the blade, using longer sweeps than you would with a jig.

LOCATE lake trout in deep water with a vibrating blade. After jigging vertically on bottom, reel the lure rapidly upward. Stop to jig every 10 to 20 feet. Lakers often follow the lure, striking near the surface.

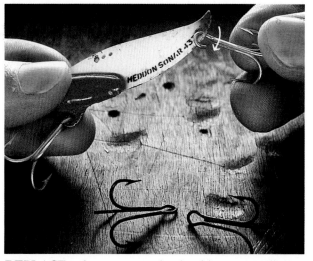

REPLACE a bent or rusty hook with a new split-eye hook by placing the free end of the eye into the attachment hole, then twisting the hook (arrow) to close the eye. Or, substitute a split-ring and a standard treble.

## Fishing With Tailspins

Originally, the tailspin was designed for bass fishing in southern reservoirs. But many fishermen have found it effective in northern waters for bass, walleyes and even lake trout.

Because the spinner blade on the tail turns while the lure is moving forward or sinking, it provides constant flash. The blade slows the sink rate, so fish have plenty of time to strike.

You can jig a tailspin vertically alongside cover like standing trees and bridge pilings, or along steep structure like cliffs and submerged creek banks. Or, you can jig it vertically while drifting with the wind or current.

Because of its aerodynamic shape, a tailspin excels for long-distance casting. Many reservoir fishermen carry an extra rod rigged with a tailspin in case a school of largemouths, white bass or stripers suddenly breaks the surface.

Fishermen use tailspins weighing from ¼ to ½ ounce for white bass and crappies; ½ to ¾ ounce for largemouth, smallmouth, and spotted bass; and ¾ to 1 ounce for stripers.

CAST a tailspin past a surface school of white bass, largemouths or stripers. Hold your rod tip high and reel

Wind Direction

ATTACH a tailspin by tying your line directly to the eye. No snap or swivel is needed, because the lure does not wiggle or spin.

JIG a tailspin vertically as you drift with the wind. Raise the rod just fast enough to feel the beat of the spinner blade. Keep the line tight enough so that you also feel the beat while lowering the lure. As you drift, adjust the line length to keep the lure close to bottom.

rapidly so the lure does not sink below the fish. When you no longer see fish breaking the surface, the school has probably sounded. If this happens, let the lure sink a few seconds before starting your retrieve.

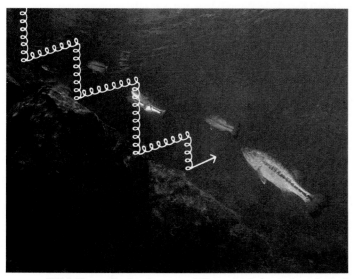

WALK a tailspin down a cliff to catch largemouth and spotted bass. Cast as close to the cliff as possible and let out line until the lure bumps a ledge or rock. Then, pull sharply to lift the lure, release line and lower it again.

REEL a tailspin steadily, just fast enough to keep it above bottom obstructions like logs and brush. The spinning blade provides enough lift so the lure can be retrieved slowly without plummeting to bottom.

# Ice Fishing With Jigging Lures

Veteran ice fishermen know that lures jigged vertically will often produce more fish than live bait. The jigging action seems to draw strikes from fish that are inactive because of the near-freezing water.

Lures designed specifically for ice fishing are usually the best choice, but you can also jig through the ice with spoons, jigs and vibrating blades. And, many anglers have found that ice fishing lures work equally well in open water. Jigging lures designed for ice fishing include the following classes:

SIDE-PLANING LURES. These lures are designed to dart sideways or move in a wide arc. This makes it possible for the fisherman to cover a much larger area than he could with live bait or other lures. Side-planing lures work well for walleyes, northern pike, crappies, white bass, and most species of trout.

A jigging minnow has a cylindrical lead body with a single hook molded in each end, a fin at one end and an attachment eye in the middle of the back. When you pull upward, the fin causes the lure to swim to the side. Jigging minnows should be tied directly to the line.

Jigging spoons designed for ice fishing are similar to those used in open water, although most are smaller and narrower. These lures have little action when pulled upward, but tumble to the side when allowed to sink with slack line. Anglers often tip these lures with whole or cut minnows, or fish eyes. Jigging spoons should be attached with a split ring.

An airplane jig is simply a lead-head jig with wings molded into the sides of the head. The lure swims in a wide circle when jigged. Tipping with minnows usually makes these lures more effective. Airplane jigs should be tied directly to the line.

TEARDROPS AND ICE FLIES. These tiny lures are intended mainly for panfish. Teardrops get their name from the shape of the body, although many are disc-shaped or round. A typical teardrop consists simply of a painted lead body molded around a #8 to 12 fine-wire hook.

Ice flies have a small lead body dressed with hair, feathers or rubber legs. The dressing gives a lifelike appearance and adds action when you jig the lure.

Teardrops and ice flies normally work best when tipped with live bait such as waxworms, mousies, silver wigglers, goldenrod grubs, small minnows or worms. Some teardrops come with soft plastic bodies that imitate grubworms.

JIGGING LURES for ice fishing include *side-planers,* like: (1) Jigging Rapala®, (2) Jig-A-Whopper, (3) Pilkki, (4) Thing-Ama-Jig®, (5) Jig-A-Spoon, (6) Rembrandt, (7) Swedish Pimple®, (8) Do-Jigger, (9) Port Clinton, (10) Geno's Jigger, (11) Russian Hook, (12) Air-Plane. *Teardrops and ice flies* include: (13) Fairy, (14) Speck, (15) Two in One, (16) Tally, (17) Barbless Purist, (18) Mini-Grub, (19) Chippy, (20) Jiggly, (21) Purist, (22) Tear Drop, (23) Ball-O-Fire, (24) Live Bait Bug, (25) Daphnia, (26) Moon Glitter, (27) Mitzi Ditzi, (28) Zip Minnie, (29) 3-D, (30) Carlson, (31) Panti® Ant, (32) Timberwolf, (33) Bomber, (34) Rub-R-Legs, (35) Do Doo, (36) Skin Yas.

## How to Use Jigging Minnows and Spoons

PULL a jigging minnow sharply upward with a twitch of your rod. The line will move to one side of the hole, then gradually settle back. Wait for the line to stop moving, then give another sharp twitch.

DROP the rod tip rapidly when using a jigging spoon. With slack line, the lure will flutter erratically downward and to the side. Wait for your line to settle, lift the lure a few feet, then drop it again.

## How to Use an Airplane Jig

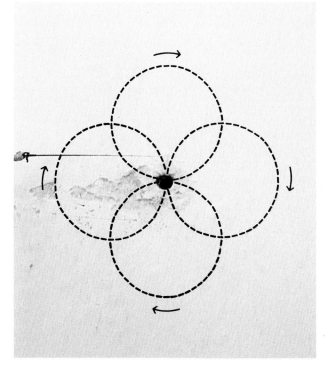

SWEEP your rod upward to make an airplane jig move in a circle. A spinning or casting rod enables you to make a sweep as long as 10 feet. Let the lure settle, pause a few seconds, then make another sweep.

KEEP jigging so that the lure moves around the hole in changing circles. For lake trout or other fish that suspend, start jigging near bottom, continue a minute or two, then move the lure upward at 10-foot intervals.

110

PAUSE for several seconds after the lure has settled when using a jigging minnow or spoon. Most fish strike after the lure stops moving. Many anglers work the lure too rapidly, not pausing long enough for fish to strike.

CONTINUE working a jigging minnow or spoon so that the lure covers the entire area around the hole (dotted lines). Both lures move outward in a slightly different path with each jigging stroke, then settle back to center.

## How to Use a Teardrop or Ice Fly

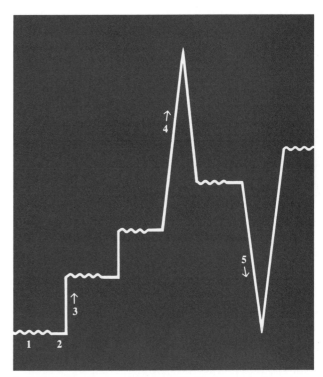

JIG a teardrop or ice fly using a short, flexible jigglestick and 2- to 4-pound-test line. Many experts prefer a spring on the rod tip, called a *spring bobber,* to a standard float. The spring helps detect subtle strikes.

LOWER the lure to bottom, (1) jig it gently for a few seconds, then (2) pause. (3) Lift it a short distance, jig, then pause again. Continue lifting and jigging. Occasionally (4) sweep the lure higher or (5) let it drop.

# Spoons

# Spoons

The flashy, wobbling motion of a spoon imitates that of a fleeing or crippled minnow, triggering strikes from most species of gamefish. Spoons work best for large predators like northern pike, muskies, largemouth bass, salmon and trout. Because spoons appeal mainly to the sense of sight, they work best in relatively clear waters.

The long-standing popularity of spoons results not only from their nearly universal appeal to gamefish, but also from the relative ease of using them. Anglers normally fish spoons far enough above bottom so that snags are not a problem. And a fish usually hooks itself when it grabs a spoon.

Spoons are generally made of hard metal, either steel or brass. A few are made of tough plastic. Because one side is concave, a spoon catches water when retrieved and wobbles from side to side.

How a spoon wobbles depends on its shape and thickness. A long spoon usually has a wider side-to-side action than a short spoon. A deeply concave spoon catches more water and thus wobbles more widely than a flatter spoon. Thin spoons tend to wobble more than thick ones.

But thick spoons have some advantages. The extra weight makes them cast better, sink faster and run deeper than thin spoons.

Most spoons have a polished metal surface on at least one side. Sunlight reflecting off this surface makes the spoon visible for a long distance, especially in clear water. Some spoons have a hammered surface that scatters light in all directions, much the way the scales of a baitfish scatter light. High-quality spoons sometimes have a plated surface that reflects more light than the duller surface of cheaper spoons.

Spoons fall into three basic categories. *Standard spoons* include any non-weedless spoon heavy enough to cast. *Trolling spoons* are so thin that they are not practical for casting. Most standard and trolling spoons have a single or treble hook attached to one end with a split-ring. *Weedless spoons* usually have some type of weedguard to prevent the fixed single hook from fouling in weeds, brush or debris.

The main consideration in fishing a spoon is how fast you work it. A spoon will not wobble properly if fished too slowly or too fast. You must experiment to find the precise speed at which each spoon performs best.

Most anglers prefer light- to medium-power spinning or bait-casting tackle when fishing with spoons. Ultra-sensitive rods are not necessary. Because fish tend to hook themselves on spoons, you need not be concerned about detecting strikes.

Spoons work best when fished with light monofilament. Heavy line restricts the wobble and is more visible to fish in clear water.

WATCH your spoon while reeling it in or trolling it alongside your boat. If the spoon slips through the water with little wobble (top), it is moving too slowly. If it wobbles enticingly from side to side (bottom), the speed is just right. If it spins, it is moving too fast.

SELECT the size of your spoon based on the size of the baitfish. It should be about as long as the baitfish's body excluding its tail.

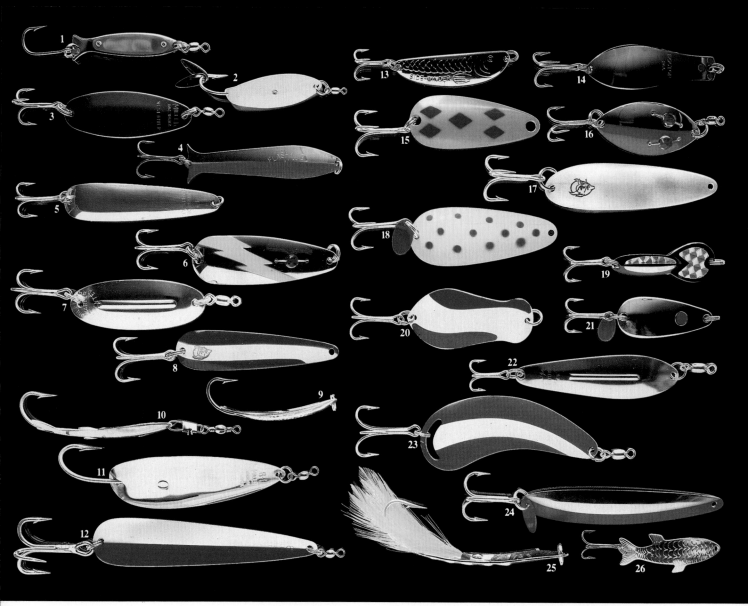

SPOONS include *thin spoons*, like: (1) Chromaglo Demon, (2) S.S.T.™, (3) Miller West River™, (4) Flash-King, (5) Sutton® 44, (6) Evil Eye™, (7) Williams Wabler, (8) Thindevle®, (9) Hammered Spoon®, (10) Gudespoon, (11) Trouter™, (12) Northern™. *Medium spoons* include: (13)

Side-Winder, (14) Doctor®, (15) Len Thompson Five-of-Diamonds, (16) Red Eye Wiggler®, (17) Cop-E-Cat®, (18) Aqua™, (19) Loco™, (20) K.B. Spoon®, (21) Hot Rod®, (22) Junior Whitefish, (23) Fishdevil, (24) Coho-Laker Taker, (25) Reflecto®, (26) Phoebe®, (27) Tony's Spoon, (28) Silver

# Standard Spoons

Standard spoons come in a confusing array of sizes, shapes and thicknesses. You can greatly improve your fishing success by learning which spoons work best for the fish you pursue and the situations you typically encounter.

The major concern in choosing standard spoons is thickness. Some manufacturers make the same design in thick, medium and thin models.

Thick spoons wobble best when retrieved rapidly. They can be cast long distances, even in a strong wind. These qualities make them ideal for exploratory fishing. When you are not sure where to find

the fish, thick spoons enable you to search out a large area quickly.

A thick spoon sinks rapidly and holds its depth when retrieved. For these reasons, it is a good choice for fishing in deep water or fast current.

Thin spoons wobble attractively at slow speeds, so they work well in cold water or whenever fish are sluggish and reluctant to strike. But you cannot cast a thin spoon nearly as far or as accurately as a thick one. Thin spoons sink slowly and tend to climb on the retrieve, so they are best-suited to fishing in shallow water.

Medium-thickness spoons perform best at moderate speeds. You can cast them easily. They sink fairly fast and hold their depth reasonably well. Because they work well in a wide variety of situations, they are the most popular of all spoons.

Streaker™, (29) Skeeter®, (30) Water Demon, (31) Dar-
devle Imp Klicker®, (32) Pops Topwater, (33) Silver
Bullet™, (34) Finsel™, (35) Pet®, (36) Sprite®, (37) Rattle-
snake™, (38) Super Duper®, (39) Syclops™, (40) Gordy G.
*Thick spoons* include: (41) Kastmaster®, (42) Swedish Ol'

Wive, (43) Limpet™, (44) Fiord, (45) Krocodile®, (46)
Spooner™, (47) K.O. Wobbler, (48) Lucky-Glo™, (49)
Wob-L-Rite, (50) Pixee™, (51) Hot Shot®, (52) Hus-Lure™,
(53) Tor-P-Do™, (54) Mr. Champ®, (55) Little Cleo, (56)
Kamlooper, (57) Rok't-Devlet®.

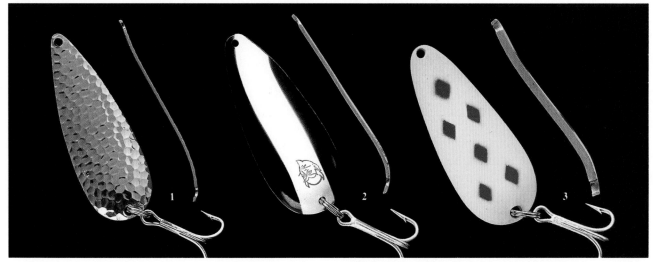

STANDARD SPOONS come in a variety of thicknesses.
A (1) thin spoon 3 inches long weighs about ⅜ ounce; a

(2) medium spoon of the same length, about ¾ ounce; a
(3) thick spoon, approximately 1½ ounces.

## Fishing With Standard Spoons

Fishermen use standard spoons for everything from long-distance casting off piers, to trolling in deep water, to stationary fluttering in current. This versatility, along with the simplicity of using these lures, accounts for their widespread popularity.

Although standard spoons are easy to use, many anglers make mistakes which cost them fish. Common errors include tying the line directly to the attachment hole, failing to use a swivel, and retrieving at the wrong speed or depth.

If the spoon does not come with an attachment ring or rounded snap, you should add one. If you tie monofilament directly to the hole, the spoon will not wobble freely and the sharp edge will probably sever the line. To avoid severe line twist, always use a good swivel, preferably the ball-bearing type.

It pays to carry a selection of thick, medium and thin spoons. The most productive depth and retrieve speed may change from day to day depending on variables like wind, cloud cover and mood of the fish. With a selection of spoons of different thicknesses, you can alter your strategy to suit the conditions.

The techniques shown on the following pages specify thick or thin spoons. But in most instances, they will also work with medium-thickness spoons.

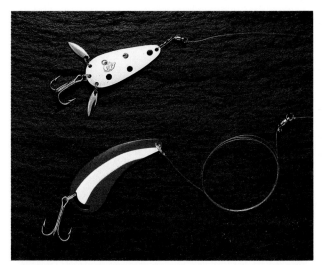

CLIP a snap-swivel directly to the hole or attachment ring. When attaching thin spoons, some fishermen prefer to splice a barrel swivel into the line 6 inches to 3 feet ahead of the lure. This prevents the swivel from interfering with the action of the spoon.

*How to Fish Thick Spoons From a Pier or Steep Shoreline*

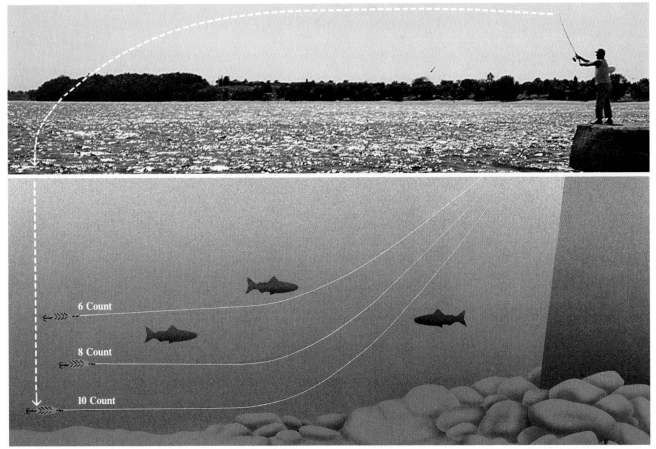

6 Count

8 Count

10 Count

CAST a thick spoon using a 7- to 9-foot, long-handled spinning rod. A two-handed cast will give you maximum distance. To locate salmon, trout and other fish that suspend, count the spoon down to different depths after each cast. Pay out line as the spoon sinks, counting until the line goes slack. Then, reel in steadily. If the spoon hits bottom on a 10-count on the first cast, count down to 8 on the second cast, 6 on the third, etc. Remember the count on each cast; if you hook a fish, count down to the same depth on the next cast.

*Other Ways to Fish Thick Spoons*

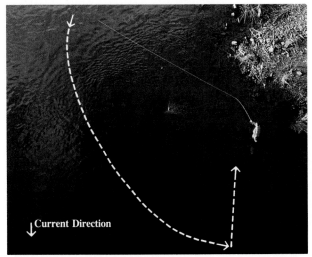

↓Current Direction

ANGLE your casts upstream in deep current. Hold your rod tip high, following the spoon as it drifts and sinks. Reel just fast enough to keep a taut line. When the spoon is directly downstream, lower your rod and retrieve with twitches to imitate a minnow struggling upstream.

RETRIEVE with sharp jerks after casting beyond a surface school of white bass, stripers or largemouths. The jerky retrieve draws strikes because the spoon acts like a shad trying to escape. Pause occasionally to let the spoon sink; the largest fish often stay deepest.

## How to Fish Thin Spoons in Current

CAST across current so the spoon alights just beyond and upstream of a boulder. Work the spoon along the upstream and near sides. Next, cast beyond and below the boulder and reel quickly into the eddy. Keep the spoon wobbling there for a few seconds, then try another spot.

POSITION yourself upstream from hard-to-reach cover like an overhanging limb or undercut bank. Cast your spoon so it alights just upstream from the cover. Let the spoon drift into the spot, then hold it in place so it flutters in the current.

## Other Ways to Fish Thin Spoons

FAN-CAST a thin spoon over a shallow flat. Reel steadily, keeping the spoon just off bottom. This technique works well for trout and salmon near stream mouths, for lake trout along rocky shorelines after ice-out, and for northern pike in mud-bottomed bays in early spring.

RETRIEVE a thin spoon just above submerged vegetation. If you feel the spoon touching the weed tips, pull sharply to free it and to make it run shallower. Largemouths or northern pike lurking in the weeds will leave cover to grab the spoon.

## Tips for Using Standard Spoons

REPLACE the treble hook with a Siwash hook if you are losing too many fish. A Siwash penetrates deeper and holds better. To make your spoon run shallower, substitute a treble hook dressed with bucktail.

REVERSE a spoon by removing the hook from the split-ring and attaching it to the ring on the other end. The reversal changes the amount of wobble and may even change the depth at which the spoon runs.

SHINE tarnished spoons by using baking soda on a damp cloth. Or, you can use metal polish, or polishing compound used for cars. If the spoon is badly tarnished or rusted, you may have to polish it with fine steel wool. A shinier spoon reflects more light, making it visible to fish at a greater distance.

ADD tape to your spoon to change its appearance. Prism tape and fluorescent tape work especially well; a thin strip often makes a big difference. Or, you can color the spoon with fluorescent spray paint. Many fishermen carry small spray cans in their tackle boxes. You may have to use a white primer before applying the fluorescent paint. Waterproof marking pens can also be effective, but the color they produce is never as intense as paint. These techniques eliminate the need to carry dozens of different-colored spoons.

# Trolling Spoons

Trolling spoons rank among the top lures for trophy salmon and lake trout. The slow, fluttering action often tempts big fish to strike at times when they ignore faster moving lures.

You can troll with any type of spoon, but trolling spoons were designed specifically for that purpose. Without added weight, a trolling spoon could be cast no more than a few feet and would plane to the surface when retrieved.

The fluttering, wide-swimming action of a trolling spoon results from the ultra-thin design. Thicker spoons have less side-to-side action at slow speeds because the force of moving water has less effect on a heavier object of the same size and shape.

Because of the ultra-thin metal, trolling spoons are less durable than other types of spoons. They often become badly bent in the process of unhooking fish. Occasionally, a fisherman retrieves the spoon and finds a sharp bend in it, the result of a fish grabbing the spoon but missing the hook. But you can return most trolling spoons to their original shape simply by bending them with your fingers.

The extremely light weight of a trolling spoon makes it relatively snagless, even when trolled over a rocky bottom. Heavier spoons sink quickly when you slow down, and often wedge between the rocks. Trolling spoons sink much more slowly. If they do touch bottom, they seldom wedge in place. Their resistance to snagging makes them a good choice for bottom-hugging fish like lake trout.

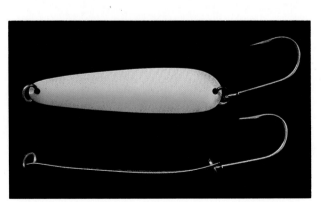

TROLLING SPOONS are thinner than any other type of spoon. A typical 3-inch trolling spoon weighs about ⅛ ounce, but some ultra-thin models of the same length weigh as little as 1/16 ounce. Many trolling spoons come with large Siwash hooks rather than treble hooks.

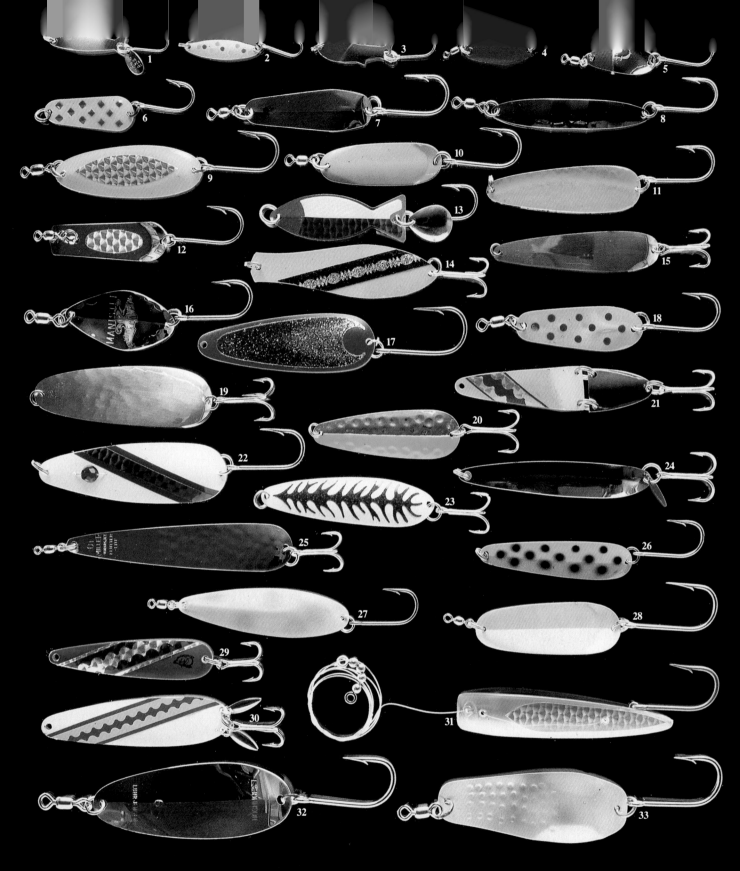

TROLLING SPOONS include: (1) Kokanee King™, (2) Needle Fish®, (3) Teaser™, (4) Red Magic, (5) Canadian Wonder®, (6) Alpena Diamond™, (7) McMahon®, (8) Candlefish, (9) Scalelite® Wobbler, (10) Salmon Seeker™, (11) Looter, (12) Pt. Defiance™, (13) Coho Joe, (14) Salmon Doctor®, (15) Sutton® 31, (16) Manistee™, (17) Coho Flasher, (18) Tom Mack®, (19) Sutton® 88HT, (20) Fin Weaver, (21) Salmon Slammer, (22) Evil Eye™, (23) Hookster™, (24) Coho-Laker Taker, (25) Flutter-Lite™, (26) Flutter Spoon™, (27) King Fish, (28) Andy Reeker®, (29) Junior Flutterdevle®, (30) Northport Nailer, (31) Apex™, (32) L.G. Johnson®, (33) Superior®.

Lures shown ½ actual size

## Fishing With Trolling Spoons

While trolling spoons have a special appeal to lake trout and salmon, they will also catch lake-dwelling rainbow and brown trout. Some fishermen use trolling spoons to search for striped bass in sprawling southern reservoirs.

You can troll these spoons without added weight when fish are near the surface. But you will need sinkers or some type of deep-trolling device when fish are deeper. Most anglers prefer downriggers so they can precisely control the depth. But many troll with wire or lead-core line, or use diving planes.

With these lures, trolling speed is critical. Some fishermen tie a pilot lure (page 69) to their boat to monitor their speed. But a trolling-speed indicator (page 68) will give you a precise reading and is easier to use. Run the spoon alongside the boat to determine the proper speed, then continue at that speed once you start fishing.

An erratic trolling path generally works better than a straight one. If you troll in an *S*-pattern, the spoon will slow down and drop as you begin to turn, speed up and climb as you straighten out, then slow and drop again as you turn the other way. The change of speed, depth, and direction often triggers a strike.

Trolling spoons wobble best when fished with light, limp line. Stiff line restricts the action more than it would with a thicker spoon.

WIRE-LINING with trolling spoons works well for deepwater fish like lake trout. Wire has little water resistance and does not stretch, so you can easily reach bottom and feel strikes. To tie a wire-line rig (inset) attach a 5-foot leader of 10-pound mono to one eye of a 3-way swivel. Tie a 10- to 16-ounce lead ball to another eye with 2 feet of 15-pound mono. Attach 20- to 30-pound wire line to the third eye with a haywire twist (page 14).

## How to Stack Trolling Spoons on a Downrigger Cable

LET OUT about 50 feet of line, make a loop with at least six twists, then attach the loop to a release above the cannonball. Keep a sliding release (arrow) clipped to the downrigger arm, then lower the cannonball 10 to 15 feet.

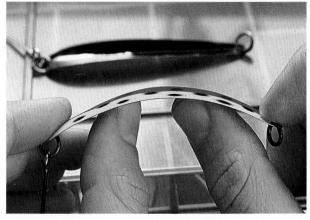

CLIP the sliding release to the downrigger cable after letting out the second line and attaching it to the sliding release. Do not attempt to stack a heavy trolling spoon on top of a light one.

LOWER the cannonball to the desired depth with both reels in free-spool and the clickers on. Reel up as much slack as possible. Slack line increases the chances of a fish throwing the hook after it strikes.

## How to Bend a Trolling Spoon to Improve Its Action

BEND a spoon by putting your thumbs together at its center, then sliding them outward while exerting pressure. The bend should be as smooth as possible. Be careful not to kink the spoon.

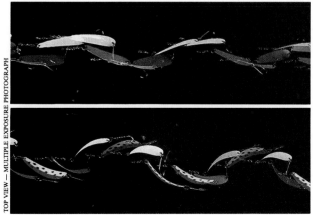

ACTION of a normal spoon (top) differs greatly from that of a bent spoon (bottom). The bent spoon catches more water, causing it to veer more sharply to the side and creating a wider wobble.

125

# Weedless Spoons

A weedless spoon can snake through weeds, brush, timber or other obstructions sure to foul most other types of lures.

Conventional weedless spoons sink rapidly, so they are a good choice for retrieving through submerged vegetation. They wobble best at moderate speed.

Spinner-spoons work better than other types when fish have difficulty seeing the lure because of the dense cover. Because the spinner or propeller provides lift, these spoons can be retrieved slowly without sinking. And fish like bass and northern pike quickly zero in on the surface commotion.

Spoons with upturned lips and plastic spoons slide across the surface more easily than other weedless spoons, so they are the best choice for fishing over thick surface vegetation. These spoons should be retrieved slowly. However, some spoons with upturned lips sink rapidly. They can be fished much deeper and should be retrieved at moderate speed.

Generally, weedless spoons are used with a plastic or pork-rind trailer. The trailer adds action, slows the sink rate and helps prevent the lure from spinning.

Weedless spoons have one major drawback. The weedguard and the large, thick hook make hooking fish more difficult than with other types of spoons. To improve your chances, carry a hook file and keep your hooks sharp.

Setting the hook is easiest with a stiff rod and strong line. To prevent your line from fraying on weed stems, use abrasion-resistant mono, usually 15- to 20-pound test.

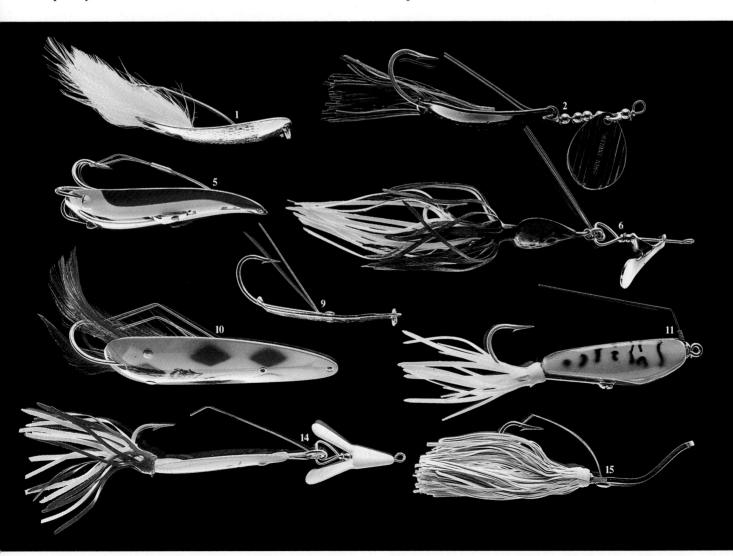

POPULAR WEEDLESS SPOONS include: (1) Hopkins Hammered Spoon®, (2) Timber Spin, (3) Jaw-Breaker, (4) Silver Minnow®, (5) Fishtrap, (6) Hawaiian Wiggler®, (7) Johnny O'Neil's Weed-Wing, (8) Herb's Dilly™, (9)

BASIC TYPES include (1) conventional weedless spoons, which resemble standard spoons; (2) spinner-spoons, with some type of spinner or propeller for extra lift; (3) spoons with an upturned lip; and (4) plastic spoons, with a wide, lightweight body. Most weedless spoons have a rigid single hook and a metal, plastic or bristle weedguard.

TRAILERS for weedless spoons include: (1) Ripple Rind, (2) Twin Tail, (3) Pork Frog, (4) plastic worm, (5) plastic frog, (6) grub tail, (7) live-rubber skirt, (8) vinyl skirt.

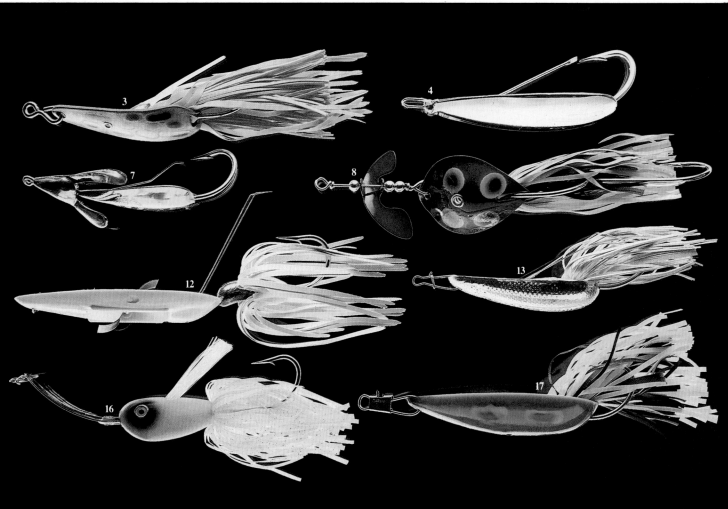

Lures shown ¾ actual size

Reflecto Spoon, (10) Feathered Weedless Dardevle®, (11) Sugarwood Spoon, (12) Weed Walker, (13) Talkin' Spoon™, (14) Hawaiian Spoon®, (15) Pork Rind Kicker, (16) Dirtybird, (17) Moss Boss™.

## Fishing With Weedless Spoons

A weedless spoon rigged with a flexible trailer has an alluring action as it slithers through the vegetation. The lures excel for largemouth bass, northern pike and pickerel in dense cover.

Because fish often have trouble locating a spoon in heavy cover, a steady retrieve generally works best, especially in unbroken expanses of weeds. An erratic retrieve will compound the problem.

Often fish will swirl or splash in an attempt to grab a weedless spoon. They frequently miss it on the first try, so you should not set the hook until you feel the strike. If you do not jerk the lure away, they will probably try again. When you do set the hook, jerk as hard as you can.

Most weedless spoons are heavy and have an aerodynamic shape, so it is tempting to make long casts with them. But you will hook more fish if you keep your casts short. At long distances, line stretch makes it difficult to set the hook. And long casts are seldom necessary because fish hiding in dense cover do not spook easily.

Weedless spoons can be effective in emergent weeds as well as those below the surface. But fishing in emergent weeds can be difficult because your line may catch on the protruding stems as it settles to the water. When you try to retrieve, the spoon comes to the surface. To avoid this problem, look for alleys in the weeds and make low, flat casts. If your line still catches on the stems, shake your rod briskly to jiggle the line free.

SKIM a weedless spoon over dense surface vegetation by holding your rod tip high while reeling. Any type of weedless spoon will work, but plastic spoons or spoons with an upturned lip are easiest to keep on the surface.

RETRIEVE a conventional weedless spoon steadily through emergent weeds like bulrushes. The spoon will seldom hang up if you cast into the wind. With the stems bent toward you, the spoon can swim through more easily.

*Tips for Using Weedless Spoons*

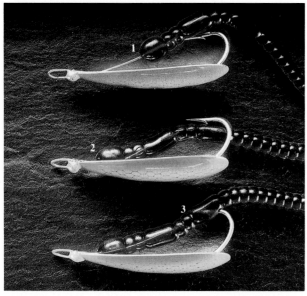

MAKE a spoon more weedless by (1) pushing a plastic worm onto the weedguard. (2) Bend the hook slightly outward so that it will penetrate the worm. Then (3) push the hook point almost through the worm.

ADD a weedless trailer hook if you are having trouble hooking fish. Push a plastic tab over the hook point, thread on the trailer, then push on another tab to hold the trailer in place.

Flies

# Flies

Most flies imitate some stage of an aquatic or terrestrial insect. Because insects are an important food at some time in the lives of virtually all gamefish, it is easy to understand why flies are so effective.

The majority of flies appeal to a fish's sense of sight, so they work best in relatively clear water. Some flies make popping or gurgling sounds, so fish can locate them even in murky water.

Flies are divided into the following classes based on the type of organism they imitate:

*Dry flies* — These flies imitate the adult forms of various aquatic insects such as mayflies, caddisflies and stoneflies. They are designed solely for fishing on the surface.

*Wet flies* — Most wet flies resemble drowned adult insects, insects just prior to hatching, or baitfish. Some brightly colored patterns work simply as attractors. Wet flies are fished below the surface.

*Nymphs* — These flies mimic the immature stages of aquatic insects. They are intended to be fished underwater or in the surface film.

*Streamers* — The elongated shape of a streamer resembles that of a baitfish. Streamers are usually fished underwater, but a few may also be fished on the surface.

*Bugs* — This category includes hard-bodied, hair and sponge bugs. These lures imitate mice, frogs, baitfish or large insects. Some draw strikes by splash and noise and resemble nothing specific in a fish's diet. Bugs are fished on the surface, or pulled beneath it and allowed to float back up.

Other flies — *Egg flies* imitate trout or salmon eggs and are fished underwater. *Terrestrials* mimic land insects like grasshoppers, crickets, ants and beetles. Some are fished underwater, some on the surface. *Trolling flies* resemble baitfish and are generally trolled in deep water. You can also buy flies that imitate common foods, like leeches and crayfish.

Most types of flies work best when attached with a Duncan loop (page 12), but dry flies are more effective when tied on with a dry fly clinch (page 15).

Learning to cast with fly tackle is somewhat more difficult than learning to use a spinning or bait-casting outfit. However, most fishermen can learn the basics of fly-casting in a few hours.

Some flies can be fished fairly well with spinning or bait-casting tackle, but you must use a plastic bubble for casting weight.

With fly-fishing tackle, the casting weight is supplied by the line rather than the lure. You must use a line heavy enough to overcome the wind resistance of the fly you select. But if the line is too heavy, it will hit the water too hard and spook fish.

The following chart gives rod- and line-weight recommendations for the major types of fly fishing.

| TYPE OF FISHING | ROD & LINE WEIGHT |
|---|---|
| General trout | #4 to 6 |
| Trout in large, fast rivers | #6 to 8 |
| Salmon and steelhead | #7 to 10 |
| Northern pike and muskie | #7 to 10 |
| Smallmouth and spotted bass | #6 to 8 |
| Largemouth bass | #7 to 9 |
| Panfish | #4 to 7 |

# Dry Flies

When fish dimple the surface on a warm summer's evening, no other lure works as well as a dry fly. Fish often refuse anything but an insect imitation when a major hatch is on.

The body of a dry fly consists of yarn, fur, feather quills, clipped deer hair or tinsel tied around a light-wire hook. The *hackle* is formed from a neck feather of a rooster. It resembles the legs of an insect and helps support the fly on the water. The majority of dry flies have a tail, made of hair or feather fibers, which also helps support the fly. Most have wings, made of feathers or hair, which make the fly more visible to the fisherman.

Dry flies come in hundreds of different designs, or *patterns*. Most patterns fall into these categories:

*Upright wing* — The most common type of dry fly, this style has standing wings resembling those of a live mayfly. The wings are usually made from feathers, hair or translucent fabric.

*Spent wing* — This type imitates a dead mayfly, which drifts on the water with its wings spread. Most have wings made of hackle tips.

*Down wing* — These flies drift with wings folded along the body, much like a caddisfly or stonefly. The wings are generally made of hair, but some are made of feather sections.

*Fan wing* — The large, curved wings are made of duck breast feathers. A fan wing does not imitate any specific insect. Because of its large wings, the fly flutters gently to the water and is easy for the fisherman to see.

*Bivisible* — Usually wingless, a bivisible fly has hackle along the body from head to tail, making it a high floater. The hackle in front is white, so the fly can be easily seen by the fisherman. The rest of the hackle is dark and imitates insect legs.

*Spider* — Another wingless fly, a spider has hackle much longer than normal and a short, slender body. It alights softly on the water and floats high.

*Parachute* — The hackle on this fly is wound around the base of the upright wing rather than around the body. Parachute flies land softly, but float low in the water, giving them a realistic appearance.

*No-hackle* — These flies have a polypropylene body that provides flotation. Most have upright or spent wings made of feathers, hair or synthetic fibers. These realistic flies work well for highly selective trout in still water or slick current. But they float so low in the water that they are difficult to see. In rough water, they will sink.

Most dry-fly patterns may be tied in *reversed* style, with the hackle at the bend of the hook, and the tail at the eye. Tied this way, a fly floats better because the hackle supports the heaviest part of the hook.

The most important consideration in choosing dry flies is to imitate the size of the hatching insect. Under most circumstances, you do not need to precisely match the shape and color.

Other considerations include buoyancy, durability, delicacy, and visibility to the fisherman.

The faster and more turbulent the water, the more difficult it is to keep your flies afloat. For best flotation, select flies with bushy hackles, and bodies or tails made of deer hair or other buoyant material. Hackles wrapped full length along the body, or *Palmer* style, also increase the buoyancy.

Flies tied with hair wings and tails are most durable. Those with feather wings, especially fan wings, or with hackle-fiber tails are most easily damaged. You need a durable fly for large fish like steelhead and salmon. When fishing is fast, a durable pattern enables you to catch many fish without changing flies.

A delicate pattern works best under conditions where fish can clearly see the fly. In extremely clear water and slow current, trout and salmon often refuse bushy patterns, because they do not closely resemble real insects. Patterns with sparse hackles and tails and slender bodies are most effective.

To know when to set the hook, you must be able to see your fly. Light-colored flies usually show up best in dim light. But you can see a dark fly better when facing into a low sun. High-floating flies are easier to see than those that ride low in the water. When fishing at night, set the hook at the sound of a rise.

TYPICAL DRY FLIES consist of (1) head, (2) hackle, (3) wings, (4) body, and (5) tail.

POPULAR STYLES of dry flies include the following: (1) upright wing, (2) spent wing, (3) down wing, (4) fan wing, (5) bivisible, (6) spider, (7) parachute, and (8) no-hackle.

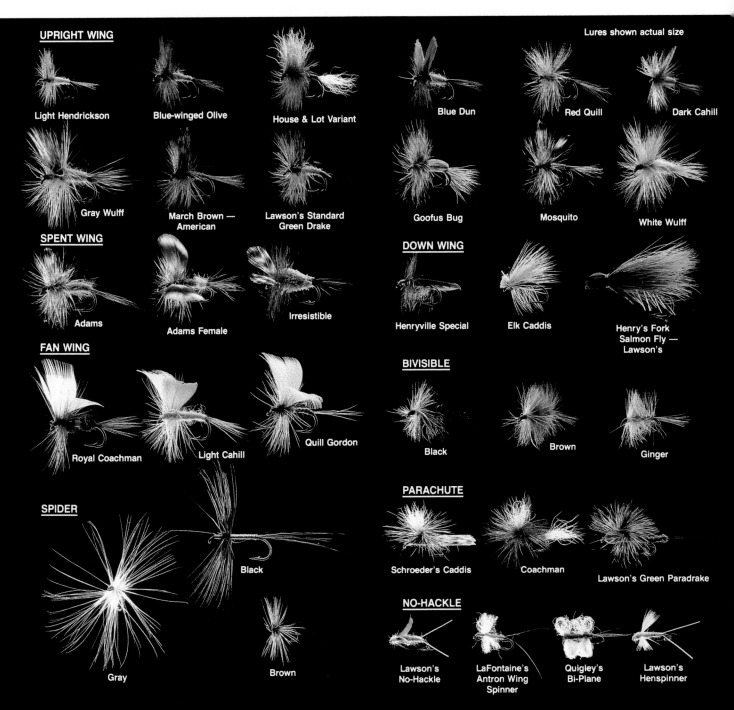

Lures shown actual size

### UPRIGHT WING

Light Hendrickson

Blue-winged Olive

House & Lot Variant

Blue Dun

Red Quill

Dark Cahill

Gray Wulff

March Brown — American

Lawson's Standard Green Drake

Goofus Bug

Mosquito

White Wulff

### SPENT WING

Adams

Adams Female

Irresistible

### DOWN WING

Henryville Special

Elk Caddis

Henry's Fork Salmon Fly — Lawson's

### FAN WING

Royal Coachman

Light Cahill

Quill Gordon

### BIVISIBLE

Black

Brown

Ginger

### PARACHUTE

Schroeder's Caddis

Coachman

Lawson's Green Paradrake

### SPIDER

Black

Gray

Brown

### NO-HACKLE

Lawson's No-Hackle

LaFontaine's Antron Wing Spinner

Quigley's Bi-Plane

Lawson's Henspinner

# Fishing With Dry Flies

The challenge in dry-fly fishing is not only to select the proper fly, but also to present it so it appears like a real insect on the water.

A lifelike presentation is most difficult in moving water. A real insect drifts at the same rate as the current. But a fly attached to a line and leader will not drift naturally unless carefully manipulated. When the line prevents the fly from drifting at the same speed as the current, fish usually refuse to strike. This unnatural pull on the fly is called *drag* and is the most common problem in dry-fly fishing.

To achieve a drag-free drift, make a *slack-line cast.* Wiggle the rod tip from side to side before the fly alights, so that the line will fall to the water in tight *S*-curves. The fly will drift without drag until current takes the slack out of the line. When the slack is gone, you can pick up the line and cast again, or *mend* the line to continue the drag-free drift.

Drag-free drifts are easiest if you keep your casts short, no longer than 40 feet. You can also minimize drag by angling your casts upstream or downstream, rather than across stream. Avoid casting directly upstream because the line will drift over the fish before the fly does. When fishing upstream, strip in line quickly enough to keep up with the speed of the current. When fishing downstream, you must feed line at the same speed as the current.

Dry flies are not always fished with a drag-free drift. Some insects, such as caddisflies and stoneflies, skitter about on the surface. When using a fly that imitates one of these insects, occasionally skip it a few inches by lifting and twitching the rod tip. Lower the rod to resume the drag-free drift.

The best time to use a dry fly is when you see fish rising. But a swirl does not necessarily mean that fish are feeding on the surface. Instead, it may indicate a fish taking larval insects below water. In this case, a wet fly or nymph would be the best choice. A true rise will leave a small bubble on the water, caused by fish sucking food from the surface.

Always cast well upstream of a rise. Remember that between rises, a fish lies several feet upstream of the spot where the rises appear. By the time a fish spots an insect and swims upward to grab it, the fish is well downstream from its lie. After it takes the insect, it returns to its original position.

On a still pool, lake or pond, try to cast so that the fly lands directly on the rise. Or, if a fish seems to be moving, watch the pattern of rises, then cast ahead to intercept it.

Trout and salmon fishermen often make the mistake of reacting too soon when a fish rises. Do not try to set the hook when you first see the rise, but wait an instant longer to be sure the fish has taken the fly.

Because dry flies are generally fished with light tippets, you must set the hook with a smooth lift of the rod. If you snap your wrist, you may break the leader. The small hook on a dry fly penetrates easily, so there is no need for a powerful hook set.

Most fishermen prefer dry flies from size 10 to 22 for trout, 10 to 12 for panfish, 2 to 8 for Atlantic salmon and steelhead, and 4 to 6 for smallmouth bass.

When fishing dry flies, always use a floating line, either weight forward or double taper. Leaders should be long, from 7½ to 15 feet.

## *How to Mend the Line for a Drag-free Drift*

Current Direction ⟶

ALLOW your fly to drift downstream until the belly in your line becomes large enough that it begins to drag the fly faster than it would normally float. You can increase the length of the drag-free drift by angling your cast farther upstream.

MEND your line by pointing your rod in the direction of the belly, then sharply flipping the rod to roll the line upstream. The belly will point upstream; the fly remains on the water. Continue the drag-free drift until the downstream belly reforms, then mend the line again.

FALSE-CAST to dry your fly after a drift. Make several casting strokes backward and forward before allowing the line and fly to settle to the water. Even when treated with floatant, a dry fly will absorb some water.

## Tips for Fishing With Dry Flies

TREAT your fly sparingly with a paste dressing for best flotation. Be sure your fly is dry before applying the dressing. If not, dry it with a powdered dessicant.

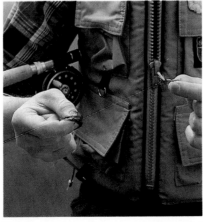

RUB mud, saliva or commercial leader-sink on your tippet to make it sink. The rest of the leader should float. A sunken tippet is less visible to fish than a floating one.

LOOK for clues that reveal the type of insect fish are eating. Inspect spots where insects collect, like spider webs and bushes. Select a fly similar to the insects you find.

# Wet Flies

Following a hatch, clouds of insects fall to the water and sink. Wet flies were designed centuries ago to imitate drowned insects, and they still work well for this purpose.

Some wet flies have no wings and imitate crustaceans, or immature aquatic insects just prior to hatching. Patterns tied with tinsel and iridescent feathers resemble minnows. Other patterns do not imitate natural food, but attract fish because of their bright colors.

The best wet flies are tied on relatively heavy hooks using soft, absorbent materials. They sink easily and the hackles and wings have a lifelike action when you twitch the fly.

The majority of wet-fly patterns fall into one of the following categories:

*Feather wing* — The wings, made of hackle tips or other feathers, imitate the wings of an adult insect. Feather-wing patterns are less durable than hair wings. But they sink faster and have more action, especially when retrieved with a jerky motion.

*Hair wing* — Some of these flies imitate adult insects or baitfish. Others are simply attractors. Because hair is buoyant, the hooks are often wrapped with wire to make the flies sink. Some have wire wound over the body or brass beads at the head. Because of their durability, hair wings work well for steelhead.

*Hackle fly* — These flies lack wings, but have a full hackle collar. They imitate immature aquatic insects. They sink quickly and have good action when twitched through still water.

*Palmer-hackle fly* — Another wingless type, these flies have hackle wound over the entire length of the body. They resemble immature aquatic or terrestrial insects, or crustaceans. Like hackle flies, they work well with a twitching retrieve.

*Salmon fly* — Most of these flies do not imitate real stream life, but rely on their bright colors to attract fish. Good salmon flies are expensive because they are difficult to tie, and many patterns call for rare materials which can no longer be legally imported.

Nymphs, streamers and bucktails are sometimes included in the broad category of wet flies because they are also fished below the surface. But each of these specialized types will be considered separately in this book.

TYPICAL WET FLIES consist of (1) head, (2) hackle at the throat, (3) swept-back wings made of feathers, (4) absorbent wool or floss body wound around a thick wire hook, (5) sparse tail made of feather fibers.

POPULAR TYPES of wet flies include: (1) feather wing, (2) hair wing, (3) hackle fly, (4) Palmer-hackle fly and (5) salmon fly. Wet flies may be fished with a (6) tiny spinner in front for extra flash.

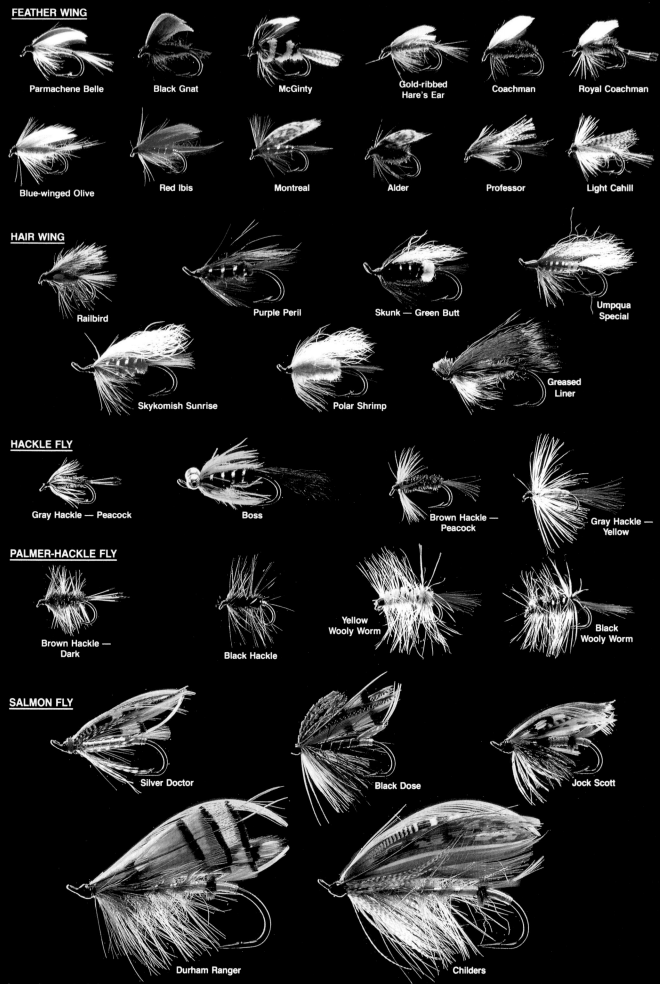

**FEATHER WING**

Parmachene Belle  Black Gnat  McGinty  Gold-ribbed Hare's Ear  Coachman  Royal Coachman

Blue-winged Olive  Red Ibis  Montreal  Alder  Professor  Light Cahill

**HAIR WING**

Railbird  Purple Peril  Skunk — Green Butt  Umpqua Special

Skykomish Sunrise  Polar Shrimp  Greased Liner

**HACKLE FLY**

Gray Hackle — Peacock  Boss  Brown Hackle — Peacock  Gray Hackle — Yellow

**PALMER-HACKLE FLY**

Brown Hackle — Dark  Black Hackle  Yellow Wooly Worm  Black Wooly Worm

**SALMON FLY**

Silver Doctor  Black Dose  Jock Scott

Durham Ranger  Childers

Lures shown actual size

CAST a wet fly along the edge of a weedbed or into a pocket to catch panfish. Let the fly sink, trying different depths to find the fish. Retrieve slowly, with long, smooth pulls or gentle twitches.

## Fishing With Wet Flies

At the turn of the century, wet flies were the only type used in North American waters. They became less popular as other types were introduced, but they remain as effective today as ever.

Wet flies are most commonly used for trout and salmon, but they work equally well for panfish, especially crappies and sunfish. Wet flies in sizes 10 to 18 work best for most trout, sizes 2 to 8 for steelhead and salmon, and sizes 8 to 12 for panfish.

Presenting a wet fly requires less finesse than other types of fly fishing. You can angle your casts upstream and mend the line if necessary for a drag-free drift, as you would when fishing a dry fly. You can also retrieve the fly across or upstream. Or, you can allow it to swing into downstream pockets on a tight line, directing the fly by pointing your rod at the spot to be fished and letting the current catch your line.

A drag-free drift is essential only when fishing a wet fly to imitate a drowned adult insect. When using flies that resemble free-swimming immature insects or small minnows, retrieve your fly across or upstream with sharp jerks. A jerky retrieve also works well in slack water.

You can also present a wet fly by *dabbling*. Simply drop your fly into an opening along a brushy bank, or dangle it next to an undercut bank to imitate an insect struggling to fly. Jiggle the fly in and out of the water, letting it sink a fraction of an inch each time. Stay low or use vegetation along the bank to conceal yourself from the fish.

To detect strikes when using a wet fly, point your rod tip at the spot where the fly lands, then follow it as it drifts. If too much slack forms, you will not be able to feel a strike. Watch the line closely and set the hook if you see a twitch or notice any hesitation. A flash below the surface may also signal a strike.

When fishing wet flies with a floating line, use a 7½- to 12-foot leader. With sink-tip or sinking lines, use shorter leaders, from 3 to 5 feet long. If you use a long leader, the line would not pull the fly as deep.

## How to Tie and Fish a Multiple Wet-fly Rig

TIE on two or more wet flies to simulate hatching insects. Attach your tippet to the leader with a blood knot, and leave about 6 inches of the heavier line untrimmed to form a dropper.

MAKE a short cast across and downstream, then hold your rod tip high, skittering the flies along the surface as they swing below you. The dropper fly bounces on the water while the other catches in the current.

## Tips for Fishing With Wet Flies

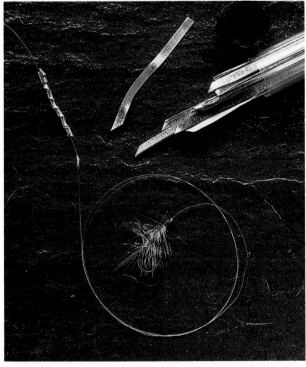

ADD twists of lead leader wrap or a split shot a few inches ahead of a wet fly for extra depth. If you need more weight, several small shot spread along the leader will cast better than one large shot.

ATTACH a clear plastic bubble to fish a wet fly with a spinning rod. The bubble provides casting weight, yet is practically invisible to fish. Position the bubble on the line according to the depth you want to fish.

# Nymphs

Most of the insects eaten by fish are immature forms. The immatures are present throughout the year, the adults for only brief periods, sometimes just a few hours. Because artificial nymphs imitate these immature forms, they catch fish at any time during the fishing season.

You can catch fish on nymphs whether or not a hatch is in progress. During a hatch, fish may feed on the immature forms swimming or crawling toward the surface rather than on the floating adults. Most anglers use dry flies when a hatch is on, but nymphs often take more fish. When the water is cold and no insects are hatching, nymphs outfish most other flies by a wide margin.

Most nymphs simulate real food organisms more closely than do wet flies. Like wet flies, nymphs are tied on relatively heavy hooks using absorbent materials, so they sink quickly. Most wet flies have wings; nymphs do not. Nymphs are sometimes diffi-

*Immature Insects and the Flies That Imitate Them*

MAYFLY NYMPHS usually have three tails. They have a single pair of wing pads and a soft, slender body. Imitations are usually tied on size 6 to 18 hooks.

STONEFLY NYMPHS have two tails, two pairs of wing pads and a relatively hard, thick body. Imitations are generally tied on size 1/0 to 12 hooks.

CADDISFLY LARVAE (top) live in cases of sand or sticks (middle). Pupae (bottom) have immature wings. Imitations, in sizes 10 to 16, resemble all three forms.

DRAGONFLY NYMPHS have a wide, flattened abdomen. They have short tails or none at all. Imitations are normally tied on size 2 to 8 hooks.

cult to distinguish from wingless wet flies. Tradition dictates how these similar patterns are classified.

Some nymphs are exact imitations, duplicating minute details of the immature forms on which the fish are feeding. Exact imitations are often tied with stiff, hard materials. Some have legs made of feather quills that have been bent, then lacquered to hold their shape. These nymphs have little action when twitched, but work well on a drag-free drift.

Other nymphs are impressionistic, suggesting the general size, shape and color of natural forms. The soft materials used in tying give them a more realistic action. These flies will work on a drag-free drift,

but are better suited to a twitching retrieve. Most expert fly fishermen prefer these impressionistic types over the exact imitations.

A few nymphs have bodies made of buoyant polypropylene yarn, so they can be fished in the surface film. These patterns, called *emergers*, imitate the immature forms as they shed their cases and transform into adults.

Nymphs are often weighted for fishing deep. Lead or copper wire wound under the body material makes the nymph sink quickly. Wire or tinsel wound over the body gives it a segmented appearance, like that of a real insect.

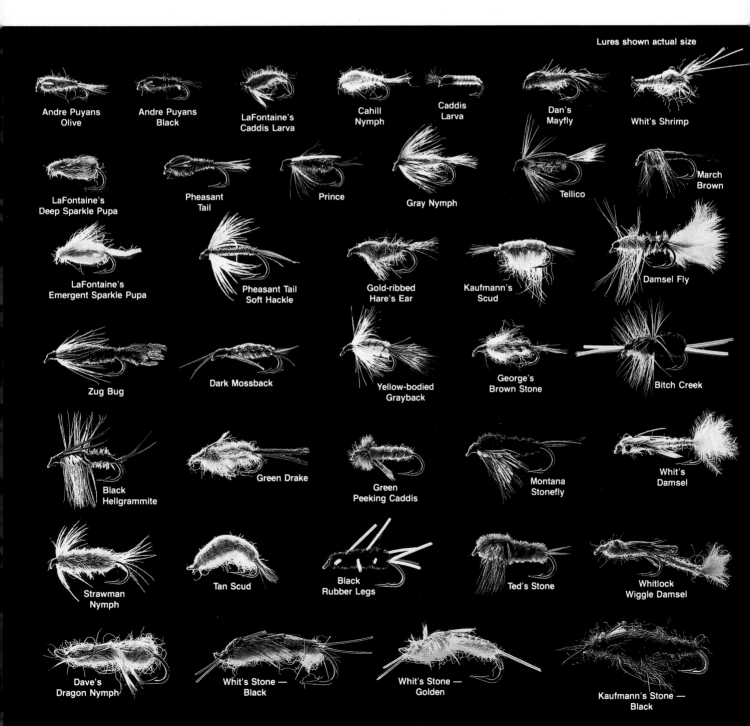

Lures shown actual size

Andre Puyans Olive

Andre Puyans Black

LaFontaine's Caddis Larva

Cahill Nymph

Caddis Larva

Dan's Mayfly

Whit's Shrimp

LaFontaine's Deep Sparkle Pupa

Pheasant Tail

Prince

Gray Nymph

Tellico

March Brown

LaFontaine's Emergent Sparkle Pupa

Pheasant Tail Soft Hackle

Gold-ribbed Hare's Ear

Kaufmann's Scud

Damsel Fly

Zug Bug

Dark Mossback

Yellow-bodied Grayback

George's Brown Stone

Bitch Creek

Black Hellgrammite

Green Drake

Green Peeking Caddis

Montana Stonefly

Whit's Damsel

Strawman Nymph

Tan Scud

Black Rubber Legs

Ted's Stone

Whitlock Wiggle Damsel

Dave's Dragon Nymph

Whit's Stone — Black

Whit's Stone — Golden

Kaufmann's Stone — Black

# Fishing With Nymphs

During the early stages of a hatch, the water often teems with immature insects struggling toward the surface and attempting to unfold their wings. If you look carefully, you may see trout or other fish swirling and flashing just beneath the surface, but not breaking water. In this situation, no other lure works as well as a nymph.

In some waters, immature insects comprise over 80 percent of the trouts' diet. Although nymphs work especially well for trout, they will also catch smallmouth and largemouth bass and most types of panfish. For trout, use nymphs in sizes 1/0 to 18; for bass, sizes 1/0 to 6; and for panfish, sizes 6 to 12.

To determine what type of nymph to use, look for natural forms in the water, on bottom, in aquatic vegetation, and on bushes or rocks along the shore. If you catch a fish, examine the stomach contents. Then select the nymph that most closely matches the prevalent insect.

Understanding how a real insect moves through the water will help you decide how to fish the imitation. Each type moves in a distinct manner. Mayfly nymphs, for example, are fair swimmers, but cannot swim against a current. In most cases, you should drift a mayfly imitation with the current or retrieve it across stream, but not upstream.

Stonefly nymphs and caddisfly larvae move about by crawling along the bottom. You can best imitate these insects by letting the current roll a weighted nymph along the bottom.

Caddisfly pupae are excellent swimmers. Prior to hatching, they swim rapidly to the surface and, with practically no hesitation, emerge into the air. Pupal imitations work well when fished with a fast-rising, bottom-to-surface retrieve. You can also use an emerger pattern dressed with floatant, fishing it in the surface film.

Dragonfly and damselfly nymphs use a jet-propulsion system to dart along bottom in search of tiny food organisms. You can best imitate their movement with a retrieve consisting of 1- to 2-inch jerks followed by pauses.

Although nymphs are often retrieved with twitches, you can fish any nymph with a drag-free drift. In most streams, fish are accustomed to feeding on immature insects that become dislodged from the bottom and drift with the current.

All nymphs can be fished in still water, including lakes, ponds, and pools in streams. Retrieve with gentle twitches or long, slow pulls. In cold water, a nymph resting motionless on bottom will often catch sluggish trout.

Nymphs are more difficult to use than most other types of flies. The major problem is detecting strikes. Often, the only indication of a strike is a slight pause or a subtle twitch. Another problem is keeping the nymph down when trying to fish near bottom in current. Avoid drag to keep your line and fly from lifting.

The lines and leaders used with nymphs are the same as those used with wet flies (page 140). Always fish emerger patterns with a floating line.

## How to Make and Use a Cork Strike Indicator

MAKE a cork strike indicator by using a hot needle to burn a hole in a cork cylinder ¼ inch long by ¼ inch in diameter. Paint the cork and peg it onto the leader butt with a toothpick. Use a floating fly line.

WATCH the cork closely; set the hook at any twitch or hesitation. Other strike indicators include a piece of red yarn tied to the leader butt, a red plastic sleeve slipped over the butt, or a tab of red adhesive foam.

MIMIC an immature insect rising to the surface to trigger strikes from trout or salmon. Position yourself upstream of a probable lie. Cast across stream so your nymph will sink nearly to the bottom before it reaches the lie. Then raise your rod tip to make the nymph swim toward the surface, simulating a rising insect.

## Tips for Fishing With Nymphs

CHECK for common nymphs by stirring up the bottom, then holding a fine-mesh net downstream; sifting through sediment with a screen; sorting through leaves, sticks or other bottom debris; or turning over rocks and logs.

DRESS all but the last few inches of your leader with silicone paste line dressing when fish are feeding on emerging insects just below the surface. This keeps your nymph slightly under the surface film.

# Streamers

Streamers differ from most other types of flies in that they imitate baitfish rather than insects. Some streamers bear a remarkable similarity to real baitfish. Others bear much less resemblance to the real thing. Instead, they attract gamefish with their bright colors and flash.

Most streamers are tied on long-shank hooks to imitate the elongated shape of a baitfish. Some have monofilament weedguards for fishing in weeds or brush. Streamers fall into these categories:

*Hackle-wing* — The wing, made of long hackle feathers, is relatively stiff. It has little action in still water but works well in current. These flies sink readily, so they can be fished fairly deep even with a floating line.

*Bucktail* — Because the wing is made of bucktail or other hair, these flies sink more slowly than hacklewings. They can be fished deep only with a sinking or sink-tip line. Like hackle-wings, bucktails lack action in still water and are used mainly in current.

*Combination* — These flies have wings of feathers and hair. They sink slightly slower than a hacklewing. Like hackle-wings and bucktails, they are best suited for moving water.

*Marabou* — The fluffy marabou wing assumes the shape of a baitfish when the fly is wet. A marabou sinks more slowly than a hackle-wing. When twitched, the fly has a pulsating action, so it works well in either still or moving water.

*Muddler* — These flies have large heads of clipped deer hair and wings of turkey quill feathers, marabou or hackle feathers. Among the most versatile of streamers, they work in still or moving water. Most muddlers float, or sink very slowly. These models are usually fished on the surface to imitate a grasshopper. But some muddlers have wire windings beneath the body material, so they sink more rapidly. These weighted models can be fished on bottom to imitate a sculpin.

*Matuka* — The hackle-feather wing is wrapped the entire length of the body with thread or tinsel. Because of this wrapping, the wing never becomes fouled in the hook bend, as it sometimes will on an ordinary hackle-wing. The matuka wing forms an upright keel, giving the fly good stability in fast water. Matukas sink at approximately the same rate as hackle-wings.

*Jigging fly* — The weighted head makes the fly sink rapidly and gives it a jigging action when retrieved in jerks. The wing is usually made of hackle feathers or a strip of rabbit fur. Because of their vigorous action, these flies work well for fishing in still water, especially for bass.

*Trolling streamer* — Used mainly for landlocked salmon and brook trout, these flies have long hackle-feather or bucktail wings. A dressed trailer hook is attached to the main hook with a short length of mono. Trolling streamers are impractical for casting because the wing would foul in the bend of the hook.

TYPICAL STREAMERS consist of (1) head, (2) cheek, (3) hackle, (4) wing, (5) body, and (6) tail.

POPULAR STREAMERS include (1) hackle-wing, (2) bucktail, (3) combination, (4) marabou, (5) muddler, (6) matuka, (7) jigging fly, (8) trolling streamer with trailer hook.

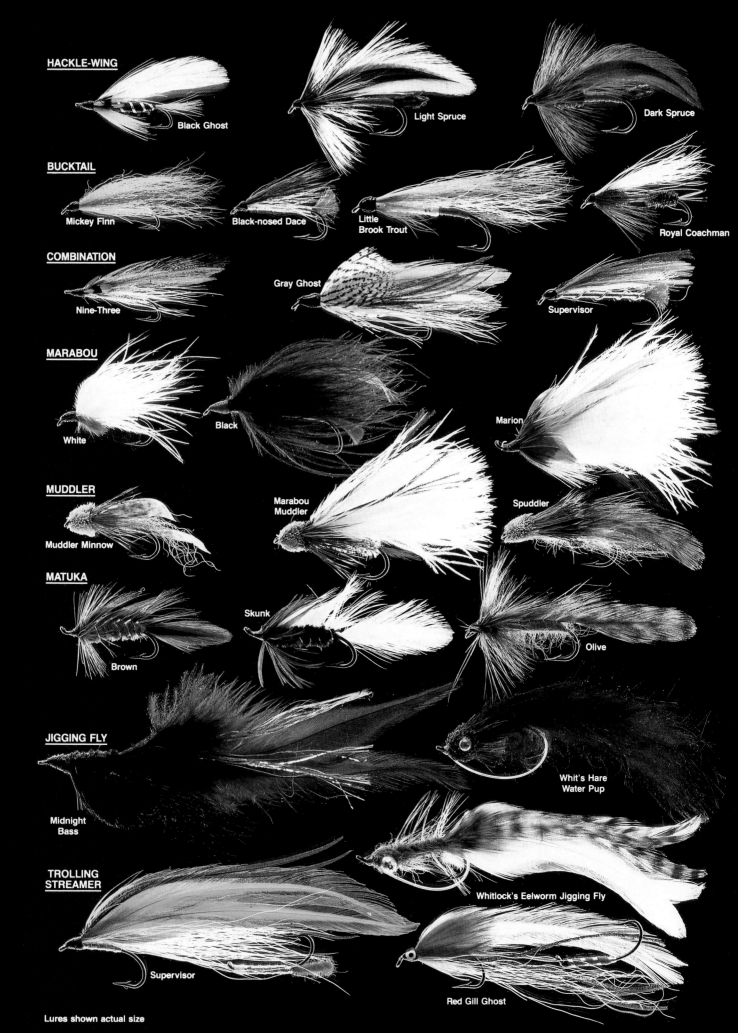

**HACKLE-WING**

Black Ghost

Light Spruce

Dark Spruce

**BUCKTAIL**

Mickey Finn

Black-nosed Dace

Little Brook Trout

Royal Coachman

**COMBINATION**

Nine-Three

Gray Ghost

Supervisor

**MARABOU**

White

Black

Marion

**MUDDLER**

Muddler Minnow

Marabou Muddler

Spuddler

**MATUKA**

Brown

Skunk

Olive

**JIGGING FLY**

Midnight Bass

Whit's Hare Water Pup

Whitlock's Eelworm Jigging Fly

**TROLLING STREAMER**

Supervisor

Red Gill Ghost

Lures shown actual size

## Fishing With Streamers

As gamefish grow larger, their diet generally includes less insects and more baitfish. This explains why streamers catch more big fish than most other types of flies.

Streamers will catch almost every major species of gamefish. Although they are often considered to be trout and salmon lures, streamers also work well for smallmouth, largemouth and spotted bass; white and striped bass; crappies; and northern pike, muskies and pickerel.

Size 4 to 10 streamers work well for most trout fishing, but you may need sizes up to 1/0 for large trout. For crappies, use sizes 6 to 12; for white, smallmouth and spotted bass, sizes 2 to 6; for largemouth bass, pickerel and salmon, sizes 1/0 to 4; for northern pike, muskies and stripers, sizes 3/0 to 2.

Because streamers imitate baitfish, you can retrieve them upstream, across stream or downstream. They can be worked fast or slow, with a steady or jerky retrieve. You can fish a weighted streamer along

bottom, skitter an unweighted model on the surface, or skate a streamer across current by attaching it with a *riffling hitch*. A fly tied with a riffling hitch has a special appeal to steelhead and salmon.

When fishing a streamer in still water, retrieve with short twitches mixed with long, darting movements. A fast, darting retrieve works well for schooling white bass or other surface-feeding fish.

Slow-trolling or drifting with streamers is an effective method for fish that suspend. Small bucktail streamers work well for crappies; trolling streamers for landlocked salmon and brook trout. Use a sinking fly line and vary the amount of trailing line as your boat moves along.

Some anglers use streamers for locating fish. Because streamers can be retrieved rapidly, they cover a lot of water quickly. Even if a fish is not interested in striking, it might make a pass at a fast-moving streamer and reveal its location. Then, you may be able to catch it with a different type of fly.

The lines and leaders used with streamers are the same as those used with wet flies (page 140). To maximize the action of a streamer, be sure to attach it with a loop knot (page 12), especially when using a jigging fly.

*How to Skate a Streamer Using a Riffling Hitch*

TIE a riffling hitch by attaching your line to the eye, then making a half-hitch just behind the head (above). Tighten the knot (below). The line should be on the side of the fly nearest you as the head faces downstream.

SKATE the streamer at an angle to the current by casting across stream, then lifting your rod tip. A fly tied with a riffling hitch creates more surface disturbance because the current strikes it broadside.

*Other Techniques for Fishing With Streamers*

IMITATE a darting baitfish using a muddler-type fly with paste floatant on the head. Use a sink-tip line and 4-foot leader. Let the tip sink to bottom, then retrieve slowly. The fly swims just off bottom, without snagging.

USE a tandem streamer rig for schooling fish such as white bass. When a fish swims off with one streamer, other fish follow in an attempt to steal the lure. Often, a following fish grabs the second streamer.

149

# Bugs

A smashing surface strike ranks as one of the most exciting moments in fishing. But excitement is not the only reason for using these topwater flies. Few other lures work as well when fish are feeding on surface foods like large insects, frogs or mice.

Many fishermen use bugs only when they see fish feeding on the surface. But these lures can be effective whenever fish are in the shallows. They work particularly well for nest-guarding fish during the spawning period.

While some bugs imitate real food, they attract fish mainly by the surface disturbance. Bugs include the following types:

*Popper* — These lures have bodies of plastic, cork, balsa wood or clipped deer hair. Most have hackle collars, and hair or feather tails. Many have rubber legs on the sides of the body. Poppers get their name from the popping sound made by the cupped or flattened face.

*Slider* — Similar to poppers, sliders have a face that is bullet-shaped rather than cupped or flattened. Sliders cause less surface disturbance than poppers, so they may work better at times when fish spook easily. Because sliders do not dig as much as other bugs, they are better suited for skittering over fast water and for slipping over lily pads or other dense surface cover. The streamlined shape of a slider makes it easier to cast than a popper, especially in windy conditions. Most sliders imitate crippled minnows on the surface.

*Diver* — These bugs are also similar to poppers, but the top of the head slopes back. The sloping head causes the lure to dive when you pull it forward. As they submerge, most divers gurgle and emit an air bubble. Divers will remain under water as long as you keep pulling them. When you pause, they float back toward the surface. These lures are excellent frog imitations.

*Sponge bug* — Used primarily for panfish, these bugs have a soft body, so fish will hold them longer than hard-bodied bugs. Most have live-rubber legs and resemble spiders. Sponge bugs float low on the water or ride just beneath the surface.

*Other bugs* — This category includes bugs that look like mice, frogs, moths, dragonflies or nothing in particular. Most are tied with clipped deer or elk hair. The hollow fibers provide excellent flotation. These flies are generally fished slowly, with slight twitches and long pauses. Some are difficult to cast because they have long hair wings that stick out sideways and cause wind resistance.

Hair bugs usually hook fish better than hard-bodied bugs. Fish hold onto hair bugs longer, giving you more time to set the hook. But hair bugs are less durable, and are harder to keep afloat because they soak up water.

When fishing in weeds or brush, choose a bug with a weedguard. The best type of weedguard is made from a heavy monofilament loop. But a weedguard reduces your hooking percentage, so you should select bugs with unprotected hooks when you will be fishing in open water.

Another consideration in selecting these lures is the size of the hook. The bend and point of the hook serve as ballast; if the hook is not large enough, the bug will often land upside down.

POPULAR BUGS include the following: (1) popper, (2) slider, (3) diver, and (4) sponge bug. Other bugs include (5) hair mouse, (6) hair frog, and (7) moth imitation with hair wings.

**POPPER**

Hula Popper

Accardo Wildcat

Scaly Popperakle

Calvert Mighty White

Bass King

Peck's Popping Minnow

Calvert Shad

Whitlock Black Peacock

Whitlock Roach

**SLIDER**

Sneaky Pete

Calvert Yellow Darter

Calvert Olive Darter

Hair-bodied Slider

**DIVER**

Frog Dahlberg Diver

Olive Fur Strip Dahlberg Diver

Purple Dahlberg Diver

Black Grizzly Dahlberg Diver

**SPONGE BUG**

Green Spider

Black Spider

Yellow Spider

White Spider

Lady Bug

**OTHER BUGS**

Whitlock Mouserat

Whitlock Wigglelegs Frog

Henshall Bug

Gerbubble Bug

Lures shown actual size

## Fishing With Bugs

A fish may take a bug with a jarring smash, but often the strike is much more subtle. Sometimes the lure seems to disappear from the surface with no noise or swirl. You must watch the lure closely and react before the fish ejects it.

To retrieve a bug, keep your rod tip low and pointed at the bug while stripping in line. If you retrieve by lifting the rod tip, your rod will be out of position to set the hook.

Most fishermen consider bugs to be largemouth bass and sunfish lures. But bugs also work well for small-mouth and spotted bass, crappies, trout, northern pike, pickerel and muskies.

For northern pike and muskies, select bugs in sizes 4/0 to 1/0; for largemouth bass and pickerel, sizes 1/0 to 2; for smallmouth and spotted bass, sizes 1 to 6; for trout, sizes 2 to 8; and for bluegills and crappies, sizes 8 to 12.

The retrieve techniques used with various types of bugs differ greatly.

Poppers can be twitched sharply to make popping sounds and bubbles. But a gentle twitch or a slight pull that just ripples the surface often works better. Fishermen commonly make the mistake of pulling the popper too far. In most cases, use the shortest tug that still makes the lure pop. Each twitch or pop is usually followed by a pause. But a fast popping retrieve, without pauses, sometimes works better for bass, pike and muskies.

Sliders can be fished with a slow, steady retrieve or a gentle stop-and-go retrieve. You can also skate a slider across the surface so it kicks up a slight spray.

A diver is more versatile than other types of bugs. You can twitch it as you would a popper; retrieve it with a short pull followed by a pause to make it gurgle, dive, then resurface; or fish it underwater by stripping in line, as you would fish a streamer.

Most other bugs work best in very shallow water. They do not make enough noise or disturbance to draw fish from the depths. Retrieve them with gentle twitches followed by pauses. These lures cover little water, so you must cast accurately to rising fish or close to weeds, brush or other likely spots.

The largest, most wind-resistant bugs may require special tackle for easy casting. Some fishermen use a powerful bass-bug rod and a bug-taper fly line (page 11). Leaders used with bugs measure from 7½ to 9 feet long.

SHORTEN the rubber legs on a popper or sponge bug if you are missing too many fish. Trimming a popper's

*Tips for Fishing With Bugs*

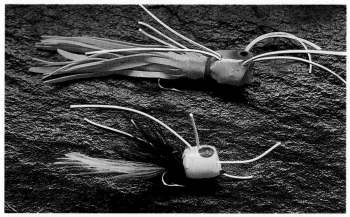

SELECT a bug with ample clearance between the body and the hook point (top) rather than one with little clearance (bottom). If the hook point extends forward past the rear of the body, you will miss too many strikes.

hackle collar may also help. Bluegills and other types of sunfish are especially difficult to hook. They continually nip at the legs or hackle collar, but do not take the lure deeply enough so that you can set the hook.

TUNE a hair-bodied popper or diver if the lure will not pop. If it skims instead of popping or diving, bend the back of the hook down. This causes the face to catch more water when you pull.

UNSNAG a bug by raising your rod tip, then snapping it downward to cast a loop of line beyond the snag. If the fly does not pull free, let the line fall to the water beyond the fly, then pull sharply.

# Special-purpose Flies

Special-purpose flies do not fit in any of the usual fly categories, but they work extremely well in specific fishing situations. Following are some popular special-purpose flies:

*Egg fly* — Intended mainly for steelhead and salmon, these simple flies are tied with fluorescent material to imitate a single egg or a cluster of eggs drifting with the current.

Fish an egg fly by angling your casts upstream, then allowing the fly to drift along bottom at the same speed as the current.

*Leech fly* — The long tail is made of marabou or a strip of chamois or latex, giving the fly an undulating action similar to that of a leech. These flies appeal mainly to bass, panfish and trout.

Work a leech fly along bottom or over weedtops by retrieving steadily or with a slight jigging motion. If you jig a marabou pattern too vigorously, the tail puffs out and does not look like a leech.

*Crayfish fly* — These flies have tufts of hair or other material tied to imitate the claws of a crayfish. They work well for crayfish feeders like smallmouth bass, spotted bass and large trout.

Drift a crayfish fly along a rocky stream bottom by casting cross-stream, then mending line (page 136). In still water, inch the fly ahead, then let it rest a few seconds. Fish often strike when the fly is motionless.

*Terrestrial fly* — These flies imitate land insects such as grasshoppers, crickets, ants and beetles. Intended mainly for trout, they are also effective for bass and panfish. When no aquatic insects are hatching, a terrestrial is a good choice.

Fish a terrestrial with a drag-free drift, either on or below the surface. Because most land insects alight near the bank, you should drift a terrestrial as close to shore as possible.

*Trolling fly* — One type, used mainly for lake trout and salmon, has a colorful mylar and hair body tied on a plastic tube through which the hook is threaded. Some have a small spinner at the tail or colored beads at the front. Another type, called a *squid,* has a brightly colored, soft plastic skirt on a plastic tube. Squids are also popular for lake trout and salmon.

Trolling flies are usually trolled with downriggers, diving planes or heavily-weighted lines. Many fishermen rig a flasher, dodger, or cowbells ahead of the fly as an attractor.

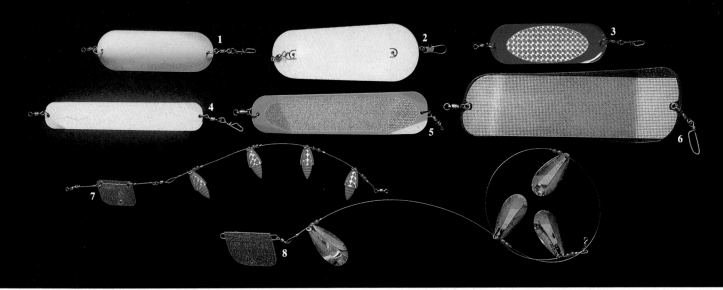

ATTRACTORS are tied 14 to 24 inches ahead of a trolling fly. *Dodgers,* which sway widely from side to side, include (1) Jensen™ Dodger, (2) King Dodger™, and (3) Herring Dodger®. *Flashers,* which rotate 360 degrees, include (4) Abe and Al®, (5) Superflasher, and (6) Hot Spot. *Cowbells* include (7) School-O-Minnows™ and (8) Flex-I-Troll®.

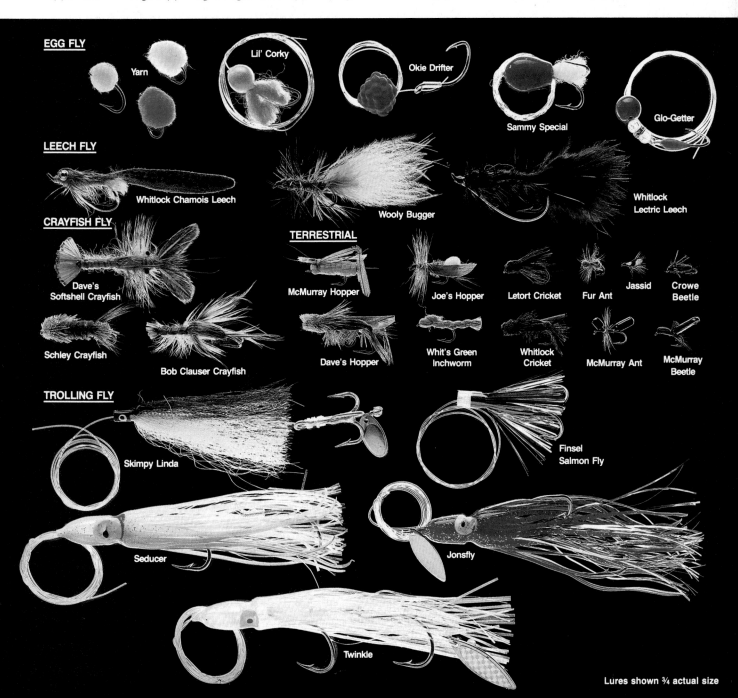

**EGG FLY**

Yarn

Lil' Corky

Okie Drifter

Sammy Special

Glo-Getter

**LEECH FLY**

Whitlock Chamois Leech

Wooly Bugger

Whitlock Lectric Leech

**CRAYFISH FLY**

Dave's Softshell Crayfish

Schley Crayfish

Bob Clauser Crayfish

**TERRESTRIAL**

McMurray Hopper

Joe's Hopper

Letort Cricket

Fur Ant

Jassid

Crowe Beetle

Dave's Hopper

Whit's Green Inchworm

Whitlock Cricket

McMurray Ant

McMurray Beetle

**TROLLING FLY**

Skimpy Linda

Finsel Salmon Fly

Seducer

Jonsfly

Twinkle

Lures shown ¾ actual size

# Index